TRUTH
TO
POWER

TRUTH
TO
POWER

JESS PHILLIPS M.P.

7 WAYS TO
CALL TIME ON B.S.

monoray

An Hachette UK Company
www.hachette.co.uk

First published in Great Britain in 2019 by Monoray, an imprint of
Octopus Publishing Group Ltd
Carmelite House, 50 Victoria Embankment,
London EC4Y 0DZ
www.octopusbooks.co.uk

Distributed in the US by Hachette Book Group
1290 Avenue of the Americas 4th and 5th Floors
New York, NY 10104

Distributed in Canada by Canadian Manda Group
664 Annette St. Toronto, Ontario, Canada M6S 2C8

ISBN 978-1-913-18301-1

A CIP catalogue record for this book is available from
the British Library.

Printed and bound in the UK.

5 7 9 10 8 6 4

To Harry, Danny, Tom and Dad

7 WAYS TO CALL TIME ON B.S.

INTRODUCTION

THERE ARE MANY THINGS I FEAR. Who I am and what I do puts me at risk. Every morning as I blink the dust of a broken night's sleep from my eyes, fumbling in the dark to turn off the tinny alarm of my mobile phone, the thing that jolts me awake and forces me to focus is the worry that I will accidentally hit the panic alarm screwed to the wall next to the headboard of my bed.

'It's all a bit dramatic in my opinion,' said my husband when they installed security measures in our home. He may very well be right. I've learned to shrug off the situation I find myself in.

Of course I worry about the death threats, of course the constant arrows that arrive on my phone, on social media, in my email and sometimes at my door pierce my skin, but this is all manageable fear. I apply a plaster to each cut, rub on a little lotion and carry on. I can risk-assess these threats, mitigate them, use the power of reason to talk myself around. The fear I cannot control, that eats me up with every passing day, is the fear of appeasement. The fear that people can be controlled by those who are more powerful, more aggressive and with a bigger voice.

For generations, brilliant crusaders have fought long, hard battles to bring us democracy that gives us citizens power. People died so that every adult would have an equal vote and an equal stake. People got together, joined arms and built the union movement, the civil rights movement and the women's rights movement. Brave activists faced riots so we could love whom we want and live freely without fear of reprisals. Martin Luther King Jr said, 'The arc of the moral universe is long, but it bends toward justice.' We have lived through progressive times because of the willingness of people to speak truth to power. So why is everything at the moment so bloody depressing? It feels as if the arc has stopped bending towards justice and has jumped into a gas-guzzling car and hit reverse. Maybe we all got used to things just getting better around us and missed out the bit where it was on us to change things. I feel as if people more than ever want to fight back and do something, but they are just not sure what that something is. People feel silenced and hopeless in the face of the powerful.

The world is a changing place – these are important times. Our politics and our lives, even in my adulthood, appear unrecognizable to the way things once were. We conned ourselves that the trailblazers of equality and human rights who went before us finished the job. Incidents such as Rosa Parks's defiance on the bus, Harvey Milk's election or the 1968 Ford Dagenham strike for equal pay for women changed the course of history for ever, it is true, but the backlash was always going to come.

Here in the twenty-first century the backlash is upon us. The far right make gains across Europe, a man recorded bragging about sexually assaulting women takes the White House, and the Chinese build encampments for their Muslim nationals. The reason all of these things can happen is because people without power feel they are powerless to speak up. We have legitimized racism and sexism in our society once again by shrugging and thinking, What's the point? Every time someone we meet or know says something questionable, we are more scared to be labelled a troublemaker than we are to find ourselves living with the trouble.

If you don't speak back to the bully, the bully always wins. I'm more scared to stand down than I am to stand up because the slings and arrows leave only temporary marks. Imagine if we capitulated on what we believe to be true and right because of fear of reprisals. The reprisals wouldn't end; they would come thicker and faster.

We have got to call time on the bullshit that makes us feel as if we are powerless, the bullshit that tells ordinary people they have a defined place in the world and should put up with their lot. The bullshit that means the same people always end up with the same jobs. The bullshit that says we just have to tolerate a rising tide of hatred and division. The bullshit that says the laws are just the way they are and you should live within a system that was designed for someone else. Wherever there is a power imbalance, such as exists between men and women, white and black people, rich and poor, boss and employee, then that power can breed oppressive behaviour. Silence and acceptance from the weaker player is the grease that keeps these wheels turning.

Forcing people to be silent and give up is the most powerful tool any oppressor has in their arsenal. 'What's the point, I won't get anywhere,' is the victory call that brings joy to the ears of every person or institution that ever sought to control you.

'What is the point in taking my boss to tribunal because he bullied me out of work? It's too much hassle and he'll probably win.'

'What's the point in reporting the bloke who groped me on the bus to the police? Nothing will get done.'

'What's the point in voting? No one listens to us anyway.'

When you utter these words, you may think that you are picking an easy life for yourself; in fact, you are picking an easy life for them.

Whether on a big global platform or just in your office, speaking truth to power is not necessarily done so that the powerful change; it is rarely that simple. Speaking truth to power is, in fact, mostly for the ears of the oppressed. It speaks to everyday people, offers them the comfort that they are not alone and gives them hope that things can change. A small act of personal resistance viewed by someone else changes the way that they feel about speaking up themselves.

I was in the park with my husband and sons recently. A woman jogged past us, lost in her own world, headphones in firmly, taking her away as she ran. Moments later she ran past three blokes sat on a bench. Unbeknownst to her, they shouted and leered, commenting on her arse and body. It didn't even register to me, which I guess says something about how I have normalized such behaviour. My husband immediately turned on his heels and walked back over to these three blokes and gave them a bollocking.

'What's wrong with you?' he asked. 'Do you think it's okay to shout shit like this about a woman who is just going about her life? Be better!' he exclaimed. Now these blokes looked sheepish but tried to keep up their bravado with something as innocuous as, 'Whatever, mate.' They had called after the woman because they could, because they assessed the situation and found themselves to be the ones with power. Thanks to my husband, who refused to be a silent bystander, they will probably think twice about doing it again, but the outcome of his intervention meant nothing to them compared to what it meant to me, my children and the other people in the park. Him standing up to them mattered to us; we all wished we'd been the one to do it, and we all saw that it was possible and nothing bad happened. He spoke up and we all grew a little bit inside.

Speaking truth to power has the effect of activation and solidarity, and this is as true in the park or in the office as it is on a global stage. If you think about the wonderful and maverick congresswoman Alexandria Ocasio-Cortez dropping truth bombs on Donald Trump as an example, she makes absolutely no material difference to his way of thinking. If anything, she makes him double down on anti-migrant policies or environmental projects. He still very much wants to build his wall. She knows this; he is not her audience, we are. Each time she speaks in Congress, she is talking to us not him; she is rallying us to her banner. She is building momentum to change things that she cannot do on her own. She makes us feel confident and safe that at least some good people are left in this crazy messed-up world. The more people who think this the more power she gets, and eventually the power shifts. Donald Trump still doesn't change his mind, but it doesn't matter when truth has turned to strength.

When I rise to my feet in parliament and sting the government with the truth about where I live or about migrant communities in my neighbourhood, they don't just say, 'Good point well made, Ms Phillips, let's change our legislation immediately. You are right, we shouldn't think that people who earn less than thirty thousand pounds are worthless. Bravo, you clever girl, consider yourself heard.' If only.

But I'm not talking to them, I'm talking to you, the regular people in the world desperate to hear someone not slagging off migrants or bowing down because things are just too hard to change. After one particularly emotional speech I made to Theresa May's face about how, thanks to her, hunger was rising in my home town, a man whose door I knocked on a few days later pulled me in to a hug and said, 'I felt like it was me standing there in parliament, that you had possessed me and said exactly what I want to say to her every time I switch on the telly.' He then asked if he could help me in any way – could he deliver leaflets or be an endorser in my literature? A man who had never been politically active other than voting felt as if he could now get up and do something.

I get that taking on world leaders is not the pursuit of most people and nor would they want it to be. Speaking truth to power does not have to be a grand thing, but what I know is that real change rarely comes from the top. Those who live in this or that bubble can have very little effect on the lives of ordinary people. I want to give you the tools to explore how you can make a change in your own life by showing how those who have been put on a pedestal for being 'brave' did it. You too can deal with the fear, the conflict and, let's be honest, the awkwardness that can come from telling your boss, your family, your neighbour that something is bullshit.

In this book we will take a look at some of those who have taken on big powerhouses, governments and multi-national companies simply because they are the most vivid examples of a David and Goliath fight, where a simple slingshot defeats a giant. But the aim of this book isn't to turn everyone into a world-famous campaigner – although if it does, I'll be chuffed – it is to help people see where unhealthy imbalances exist in all our lives and perhaps encourage you to do something about them.

If something doesn't sit right, it probably isn't right.

While writing this book I interviewed people who courageously stood up to be counted when something wasn't right. These were ordinary citizens who, when faced with calamity or the fatigue of putting up with the status quo that harmed and controlled them, decided to call time and dared to try to change things. They are all truly inspiring, although they would each wince at the suggestion. From every one of them we can learn lessons in how to speak truth to power.

What I learned from these inspirational people – and I hope you will too – is that each of us can find the courage, regardless of how we doubt ourselves. While courage is essential, it is not always enough. I hope this book inspires you to speak truth to power but also shows you how to plan the journey, how to rally people to a cause and how to use the media and platforms you can access to do that. I hope that the words of those who have done it will inspire you, of course, but it would be remiss to ignore the pitfalls and the backlash that can come from stepping forward. Every person I spoke to – and I am sure every person who ever spoke truth to power – was scared but had to keep going; most faced some sort of backlash and it is important to know how to handle fear and dissent. Overall, I hope this book shows you how to do all this and want to come back for more, because I know – and all the people I interviewed know – that changing the world, while tiring and difficult, is the greatest, most liberating feeling in the world. It is a gift.

I make no criticism of those who have not spoken truth to power when they wanted nothing more than to do so. We have all been conditioned to pipe down; it is not our fault. The women who are beaten, the kid who gives the bully the exact reaction they want or the little man who simply cannot fathom how to take on the machine are all conditioned to do so. Grooming and society teach us our place. Stay in your lane.

But my hope is that this little book might give you some inspiration to fix this. Speaking truth to power and learning to call time on bullshit is not something only those born brave do. Those who do it learned it and then keep on practising. These people are an inspiration, but there is no reason why we all can't do it.

If you believe that speaking truth to power is for the exceptional, it is because that is what the powerful told you to keep you quiet. It doesn't have to be the exception, it can be the rule that we make those with power live by. There are considerably more of us than them.

Here's how.

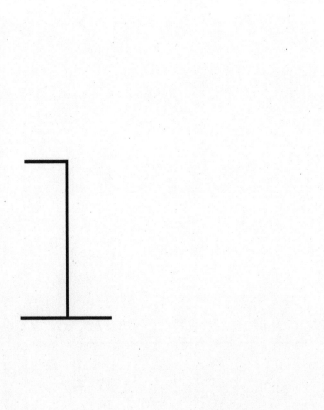

NOT ALL HEROES WEAR CAPES

EVERY SINGLE ONE of the people I interviewed for this book laughed when I asked them if they were brave. Some threw up their hands in mock horror and responded with stories about how scared they had been when they spoke truth to power. All immediately leaned on their ordinariness. Not one considered themselves a hero or to be exceptional in any way. The common refrain was: 'Most people would have done the same in my situation.' All cited other people who had helped along the way, wanting to diminish their own position as a change-maker, and all completely squirmed at the idea of being inspirational.

Funnily enough, when I told each of them about the other people I would be interviewing or had interviewed and gave a snapshot of their stories, all felt differently about those people. They all thought that the other people were brave and inspirational, responding with comments like, 'Gosh, I don't know how they coped all those years,' or, 'I could never have put up with such pressure.' Funny how people don't assess themselves as being capable, tough, brave or bold, but are happy to see it in others.

People all naturally assume that bravery describes someone else. The bravest people I have ever met, who have done the most astonishingly courageous things in the face of real danger, would have all said, had you asked them beforehand if they thought themselves capable, 'God, I could never do that.' And yet they did.

You. Can. Do. It.

It's as simple as that really. Anyone can speak truth to power. Anyone can decide that enough is enough. Anyone can be the person in a group who raises their hand and says, 'Go on then, I'll take this forward.'

There are, of course, all sorts of reasons why you may not feel best placed to have a voice that will change things. Our existing power structures mean that women, people of colour, migrants, poor people, disabled people, people not speaking their mother tongue or people whose faces just don't fit all find it hard to be heard by people with power, or by people who seem higher up the hierarchy than them.

But don't let the fact that you have previously felt unheard or ignored be your excuse for not speaking up. It was the reason the powerful ignored you in the first place, in the hope that it would make you go away. Don't go away. Stay! We need you in the battle against the bullshit.

Don't assume that fighting back is something other people do; you can and should do it.

THE ORDINARY HERO

AT THE AGE OF 22, Zelda Perkins started working for the movie company Miramax's London office, where she was put in the role of assistant to Harvey Weinstein. By her own admission, because of her upbringing and her youth, she was initially naïve about how powerful Weinstein was. Zelda is a slight, elegant woman, softly spoken with a cut-glass English accent. She had been raised by her grandparents after the sudden death of her mother when she was three years old. She had had a sober and controlled childhood in which she had grown up learning strict rules about right and wrong. Zelda was told by other women when she started the job that Weinstein could be difficult to work with and she was warned to keep out of his personal space.

One day, while working away at the Venice Film Festival in 1998, Zelda was performing her role, being a busy PA, organizing the day's meetings, when her own assistant disclosed to her that Harvey Weinstein had the night before attempted to rape her. 'I remember very vividly, she was sitting on the bathroom floor. I was sat on the floor next to her, and she was in a terrible state. Obviously, I was trying to go through the things that we could do, I said we've got to go to the police but she wouldn't. I realized I was in a situation where I could not push that hard, but I was furious and wanted to go ring bells and call for help and scream for the police.'

Zelda did not blow the whistle with the security of many dazzling Hollywood stars stepping forward with her; she spoke up against Harvey Weinstein some twenty years before any of us in the general public knew about his predilection for sexual harassment and abuse. At the age of 24, Zelda risked and in fact gave up a career most of us could never dream of having. There she was, flying off to the Venice Film Festival on a private jet, staying in a fancy hotel, mingling with the likes of Leonardo DiCaprio, when she walked up to Harvey Weinstein during a lunch with a very powerful and famous director and said, 'Harvey, you need to come with me right away.'

'I don't understand when people say to me that I was really brave, because it was not me being brave. I had no choice,' said Zelda, when I asked her what made her step up and take on her boss. For anyone, taking on your boss if you think they have done something wrong is a tough gig. If your boss is Harvey Weinstein, and he is not only in control of your employment, your financial stability, but also is one of the biggest powerbrokers in your industry, it is more than brave, it is risky.

In a junior position, most 24-year olds would not be able to find the resolve to confront their superior, but Zelda told me, 'I just went downstairs in the hotel; the only thing I was worried about was that he was in a meeting with somebody he'd been desperately trying to meet with for years. I knew that Harvey would be furious with me for interrupting him – you never ever interrupted a meeting. The only thing I was nervous about was that I would have to do it in front of the people at the table, because there was no way that I was going to walk away. I was scared he would throw a scene that would grow in such enormity. But part of me felt, well, bring it on, because then at least it'll be out in the open. He was sitting on a table outside on the terrace at the Excelsior. I tapped him on the shoulder. He turned around, beginning to look really cross. I said, "Harvey, you need to come with me right away." He did not miss a beat. He got up from the table, said, "Excuse me, I'll be back in a moment," and walked with me like a lamb. I probably went white when he did that. I felt like every bit of blood had drained from me because I knew in that moment that he was one hundred per cent guilty.'

Can you imagine the balls, the sheer chutzpah, it took to do that? Zelda is a tiny dot of a woman. Imagine the courage it took to stand up to a broad and powerful American movie mogul in front of a table of famous Hollywood film people. If I close my eyes and try to picture this, it appears in my head like a little girl standing stock-still in front of a raging bull.

What makes some people step forward? We like to think people are brave or brilliant and that they are different from us. Zelda disputes this forcefully when I insist on her immense courage, and she is right to because every single person I have met who truly stood up to be counted and pushed back against an oppressor woke up on the morning that they did it as an ordinary human being, just like you and me. Despite the apparently glamorous setting of the film festival, Zelda had just turned up for work that day, not expecting any drama and certainly not expecting to make any momentous decisions. I think she is a hero for what she did and how she dared to do it, but I also recognize that most heroes are just people who found themselves in a difficult situation and decided not to let fear instead of hope for change be their driver.

THE EXCEPTIONAL

ARE BRAVE PEOPLE wired differently?

One of the ways the powerful control us is to claim that these ordinary people who do extraordinary things are exceptions to the rule. And too often we believe it.

Folklore or propaganda that it is the brave few who get medals of valour mean the hierarchy doesn't topple. It makes us feel as if we could never do the things that Zelda did, but had Zelda been asked before she did it, before she faced her moment of reckoning, she wouldn't have thought herself capable either. Don't believe the idea of the exceptional. We all have the capacity to be brave. Any one of us can speak up.

People tell me I am brave because I stand up for myself and I am willing to speak up against those who want to control me. My classmates from school send me emails or tweets that say things like: 'You were always going to end up taking on the boss man.' My mother died when I was in my twenties and she herself had been a crusader who helped take legal action against a multinational pharmaceutical company whose drugs had irreparably damaged my grandma's eyes. Think Erin Brockovich but with a bad eighties perm and questionable dungarees. People who knew my mom say things like, 'You're a chip off the old block,' or, 'I see your mom in you every day when you are fighting the power,' and the mythology that somehow fighting injustice is a sort of *Game of Thrones*-style bloodline or something that you learn in childhood persists.

The trouble is that I sometimes believe it. Being made to feel special or different is an indulgence. As if destiny is real or that we are all in predetermined categories where some people are the battle ants and others are the worker ants. We love a story.

In truth, people like Zelda Perkins become figures of stature after the fact, not before it. A mythology begins to surround those who seize power away and show courage in difficult circumstances. The idea that some people are wired for bravery and others are not is simply not true. When Julie Hambleton heard the news that her sister Maxine had been killed in the IRA bombing in Birmingham, she was 11 years old. She went on to spend the next 45 years of her life fighting to bring to justice those who had killed her sister and the institutions that had failed to do the same.

Doreen Lawrence is one of the most down-to-earth women I have ever met. She was just an ordinary mom and bank employee who fought back against the police when they failed to properly investigate the death of her son Stephen in a racist attack because of their own racism. The first time I met her we were about to go on stage at the Labour Party Conference after she had been made a Labour Party baroness. She was absolutely terrified about making a speech. I tried to comfort her, saying, 'You're Doreen Lawrence; you could go on the stage and read out the phone book and still get a standing ovation.' In America in the 1950s, Rosa Parks was a department store worker who got on a bus and ended up being an icon of the civil rights movement.

I do not want for a second to diminish the courage of what each of these people did. I think that they are incredibly brave and inspiring and also unbelievably selfless in the face of certain heartache and trouble, but I don't think that they are fundamentally different to anyone else. Their actions have been exceptional, no doubt, but they as people were not born special, they are not wired differently.

STEPPING UP OR STAYING SILENT

SO WHY IS IT that some people do step up and some people don't? Why do some people feel that they just can't speak up, that they don't have the resources, the knowledge, the skills or the networks to do it?

Zelda Perkins tells me that when she heard what she did, she had no choice, she had to speak up, but in fact she did have a choice. She may very well have felt because of her upbringing, her morality and the criminal accusations in front of her that she had no choice, but she soon found out that others had made different choices. Others decided not to step forward, speak up or do the right thing. Other assistants and actresses had been there before her and faced similar situations and had said nothing. Zelda recounts how she tried to take forward her complaint when she returned to the UK. 'We didn't know what to do, and the victim was too scared to go to the police, especially as it had happened in a different country. The only person we told was the only direct senior I had, an executive producer I had been working with. I guess she was a case study in herself of what you have to do to become a successful woman in that industry because she did nothing, she didn't seem surprised and just said, "You get yourself a lawyer." She was not shocked when I told her what had happened, which shocked me and panicked me because I realized that I was in more of a difficult position than I'd thought.'

So why do some people choose to do it? It is true

that for those who face oppression because of cultural ills, such as racism and sexism, keeping your head down and not being the person who speaks up is understandable because they know from the experience of everyday life that their voices matter less to the powerful. No one could or should judge this; however, it is my experience that often the most willing to step up and fight back come from a discriminated background, be it that they are disabled, from a minority race, gay or a woman. They are often the bravest people because they have had more practice at shouting to be heard; your average white middle-class man often has little to struggle for and so doesn't get much practice at the struggle.

That said, regardless of what world you grew up in, for most people, being directly involved in an incident is what sparks their flame to fight back. People will often sit back when a cultural practice is wrong or injustices are passed around like gossip that is happening to someone else. For so many people who have found the courage to speak truth to power it is because a long-ignored or -tolerated cultural practice walks up to their front door and knocks on it. Your cause has a way of picking you; it is rarely the other way around.

NEVER WASTE A CRISIS

THE THING THAT IS TRUE in all the stories I have heard and all the times I have dug deep and tried to change something is that an incident occurs; it is the final straw, the crystallizing moment, but it usually follows years of concern that something isn't right. Why do we wait until someone is dead or someone is imprisoned wrongly or freed unfairly before we act? I think it is because we believe we are powerless to change things; we shrug and say it has always been this way, that we can do nothing about the machine. A trauma changes that.

When Zelda Perkins heard about the traumatic experience of her friend, her instant reaction was to act. The woman in question, the victim, was more cautious, traumatized, not sure she wanted to report it to the police. She was aware of how powerful Harvey Weinstein was and how her word against his would leave her adrift. While this is an example of a very powerful man in a very extreme situation, the decades I have worked supporting and representing victims of sexual violence has taught me that this reaction of the victim is a universal one. A person who is traumatized, belittled, overpowered often needs a champion. Zelda recalls how she dealt with this situation.

'I said to her, "Look, whatever happened, whatever you want to do, this is done for me. I can't now go on and continue working for this man, now I've heard what he's done. So, I'm finished. I'm done. And, and if you're afraid that you don't have enough power in this situation, you've got me on your side."'

Faced with the impossible challenge of standing up to a giant in her industry, Zelda Perkins – without any of the resources or knowledge that she needed – put her trust in the law. She used her crisis to drive her forwards. Unable to take a criminal case because the direct victim did not feel able, Zelda set about taking action using employment law. What she discovered was that when you are David and you only have a slingshot to defend you, regardless of the fable, Goliath usually wins. 'The lawyers told us that the only realistic option was to make a damages claim and enter into an agreement. I was told by lawyers who I thought knew better than me that it wasn't worth going to court. It was heartbreaking because I believed in justice but this was all just about money and power. He was represented by one of the best law firms and even though the allegations were criminal we were advised by our lawyers to take a non-disclosure agreement [NDA].'

It is a common scenario: the powerful seek to shut down a crisis as quickly as possible and they will use whatever means are at their disposal to do this. Think of the Hillsborough football disaster, the Grenfell Tower fire, the Yazidi women enslaved for sex by Isis, the mass shooting at Stoneman Douglas High School in Florida. In each case, the powers that be wanted to deal with things in their own way. At Hillsborough they wanted to protect themselves by shifting the blame for the deaths of innocent fans; at Grenfell they refused to accept that the issue was broader than fire safety and was about how the establishment expects some people to live. The Yazidi women were told by the US, China and Russian governments that their fight against rape as a weapon of war didn't need international monitoring systems. They were also told by their own Yazidi leaders that the children born of their rapes by Isis fighters would not be welcome back into their community. The young people from Stoneman Douglas High School were told that the fact that their friends were dead and that their lives were forever changed had nothing to do with US gun laws.

Without champions who step forward to own the crisis, the solutions of how to improve an issue in the future will belong to people who will not be affected by the change. Therefore, nothing will change for the ordinary people and, inevitably, such crises will happen again, just on a different street, in a different town. Never waste a crisis because that is what the oppressors will always do. They will tell you the problem is smaller than it is and rely on existing hierarchies to close it down. We can't let that happen.

I don't mean to sound crass – some of the tragedies and crises I am talking about in this book are not things we would want to happen to any of us. I'm aware that considering them, tools for change might appear insensitive. A common criticism of people who strive for change is that we are using tragedy for political ends. This is a silencing technique that attempts to stop us talking about wrongdoing or make us feel squeamish about highlighting injustice. Never forget that if something in your life or the lives of others is going wrong, we have every right to talk about it. Those who cause distress and crisis in our lives do not then get to tell us that we must wait in an orderly manner designed by them to feel what we feel. Speaking truth to power is so often about trying to make sure that the voices of those who are affected by a crisis are heard in its aftermath.

Power tries to survive and one of its major survival techniques is to kid people that the bad thing that happened is a one-off, an accident, an exception, not part of a pattern of something that has become the norm. The idea of an exceptional case is used again and again by people with power.

Often the powerful know they must do something if they have used their power to oppress; usually they respond with a tiny bit of piecemeal change thrown like crumbs off a table to a beggar. The NDA negotiated for Zelda and her traumatized colleague stipulated that they had to take the best endeavours to not disclose anything even in civil or criminal cases brought against Harvey Weinstein. In return for their silence, which Zelda has stated many times she felt forced to agree to, she and her colleague also made demands that Weinstein would have to attend therapy for three years, and that Miramax would be forced to inform Disney (its parent company) or fire Weinstein if any further settlements were attempted. These were the crumbs off the table they were forced to eat, because the management of their crisis had been taken out of their hands. As is always true of such offers, the powerful side did not stick to it, knowing Zelda wouldn't have any power to enforce it.

———

Zelda Perkins did the right thing; she channelled the crisis in front of her and turned it into personal courage to do something. But what failed her all those years ago was that she had neither the resources nor the knowledge about what to do next. She didn't waste the crisis, but she also didn't plan on a war that she could never have won on her own.

The crisis moment is often the thing that will turn you from a silent observer of oppression to an active warrior against it. We must channel that feeling and the brief window of sympathy and opportunity that comes of an injustice, but stepping forward in and of itself is usually not enough to change things long term. That needs persistence, planning and people. The powerful have all of those things in place already and they will attempt to use them to make authentic voices waste a crisis, to squash and limit the damages to their powerbase. Taking the first step and knowing you should is vital, but without a plan or a clear pathway through to an outcome, the path can be cut very short.

WHAT IF SOMETHING JUST FEELS WRONG?

DO YOU HAVE TO WAIT around for a crisis not to waste before you can test if your motivation is good? No, because what's really interesting is that despite their campaigns being sparked by dramatic, sometimes shocking incidents, almost always, someone somewhere had known for a long time that there had already been a problem. After the devastating fire in Grenfell Tower in West London, which killed 72 people, it emerged that issues and concerns had been raised before. In the case of the killing and investigation of the black teenager Stephen Lawrence, it was well known that the police were institutionally racist.

The startling thing for me about listening to Zelda Perkins talk about how she stood up to Harvey Weinstein and a big movie company desperate to keep secrets is that deep down she knew he was a perpetrator, because he had sexually harassed her in the three-year period that she worked for him. 'I mean, I knew that he sexually harassed me,' she told me, 'but I wasn't aware of how bad it was, which sounds ridiculous.' After the fact, she can look back and see the trends.

Work, because of its hierarchical nature, is the most obvious place where people find themselves in situations where they could change things for the better by speaking truth to power. How many times have you witnessed something at your workplace that wasn't right? How many times have you felt that someone was being treated unfairly or wondered how come everyone at the top looked the same? There are some clear issues in the workplace that most people think if they heard about it, they'd do something. Few people will ever be put in the kind of extreme situation that Zelda Perkins found herself in, but most of us probably think that if we were, we would at least try to do something. But it doesn't have to be this extreme, we can all look around at the places where we work and where we live, and think about how we could improve them.

The thing about problematic systems is that they tend to produce repetitive outcomes; it is, in fact, entirely how they are designed. There doesn't need to be an incident for people to identify a power problem. Pay is the best example of where trends have led to terrible injustices. In 1968 the 187 female sewing machinists at the Ford car plant in Dagenham went on strike over the reclassification of the firm's wage structure, which meant that women doing skilled work would be paid less than men in the same position. They were not waiting for something bad to happen before they fought back against their bosses to demand equal pay for men and women in work. If you have a niggling feeling that something isn't right at work, looking at trends is the best place to start. Have all the women at your work failed to return after their maternity leave? Is there a high staff turnover amongst black and minority ethnic people? Does your boss always employ young women in certain roles? Are there definitely people without many skills getting promoted faster than they should? Are there high rates of sickness?

My best advice is to never assume coincidence when looking at trends of wrongdoing in an institution. Coincidence is rarer than design.

WHAT'S MY MOTIVATION?

ANOTHER QUESTION that is always worth asking yourself before taking the first step is: what is your motivation? It is very important to remember your motivation when you decide to be brave. Speaking truth to power rarely changes things quickly and, in some cases, it changes nothing at all. It almost never changes the mind of the very powerful oppressor. It is for the ears of the oppressed. Zelda Perkins had to show her colleague, who was scared and afraid, that things could be better. Her motivation was giving strength to someone else.

In every interview I have undertaken and in every case in my own life when I have taken the deep breaths, closed my eyes and stepped forward, it has always been for the benefit of someone else. For some reason the justification we make with ourselves when deciding to take on a cause is always, 'I had to protect other people.' Even in the cases I have studied where the person who fought back had been the direct victim of a powerful oppressor, such as the girls abused for years by a Rotherham sexual exploitation gang or the parents who lost their children in the Hillsborough disaster, their justification for bravery and fighting the system is never self-interest. It is always for the sake of a friend, a child or future victims. People find their courage rarely in themselves but in the hope of stopping what happened to them or their loved ones from happening to other people.

'I couldn't live with myself if this had happened to even one more person.' This is the mantra of those who speak truth to power. This could seem like a burden of responsibility, and for many who dedicate their lives to an immovable feat it can be a burden, but I choose to see this statement differently. I choose to see these words as a citizen realizing their own power. It is a statement full of agency, full of drive. It has purpose and direction. I can control this, or at least I can try; and knowing that you tried for many brings some comfort for a loss or a trauma. Speaking truth to power in lots of cases provides us with recompense for a failure we have given ourselves, however unfairly.

So, your motivation matters, and it really is worth stopping for a second before you unleash your fire and asking yourself: why am I doing this and what do I hope to achieve? For most people, there will be a clear and obvious outcome: making your workplace more pleasant, changing a law that discriminates, making where you live safer. In Zelda's case, there was a workplace issue and a clear and obvious threat, in the shape of Harvey Weinstein, but the bigger structural issue she went on to discover was how the law was being used to protect predatory and bullish executives. And not just at Miramax – NDAs were being used all over the world to allow bad companies to get away with abuse and wrongdoing.

Zelda's motivation was never to punish Harvey Weinstein; it was to improve the place where she worked. Years after the incident, when she finally broke the terms of her NDA, her motivation was to shine a light on how effectively the laws we believe protect us can be used to silence us. As a result, Zelda became a lead campaigner in the battle against the use of NDAs in the cases of those who have suffered sexual harassment and abuse at work. It was never about wanting to beat Weinstein.

Spite, even when fuelled by righteousness against a powerful individual, should never be your motivation for taking the first step in what can be a long and winding road. When people become fixated on the person rather than the problem, the battle is easier to discredit as malice and bitterness, and is inevitably disappointing. 'I have come to terms with the fact that I will probably never see Harvey behind bars for what he has done, but I want to make sure that we stop people thinking it's acceptable to abuse and then silence,' Zelda says.

I sometimes encounter people in my constituency who come to me for help but seem fixated on scalping an individual. They appear less credible and are rarely satisfied, no matter what sanctions may be doled out to their aggressor. Getting back at that person rather than doing a good thing for their victims or the public becomes an obsession, and in most of the cases I have seen they appear to drink poison every day and expect it to kill someone else. Personal vendetta will not help you speak truth, but it will certainly make you feel bad. Hate the sin not the sinner.

Imagine you are at work, and Ray from accounts comes into your office to give you and your colleagues something. He hands it over and stops for a chat and tells you about what he got up to at the weekend. As usual, Ray includes a smattering of mildly racist banter in his description that makes everyone silently wince. Should you continue to be a bystander to this 'banter'? It isn't aimed at you and doesn't directly harm anyone around you in the moment, but it does make everyone feel a little bit uncomfortable and has probably in the past made your black and minority ethnic colleagues feel reticent about asking Ray for stuff, thus making their job more difficult.

You have a choice here. If you think that it would make your workplace a safer space for you and your colleagues, it is probably initially worth saying something to Ray on his own, or you could speak to his boss. Those actions might bring about change. But if your motivation is that Ray is a massive dick and you want to use personal confrontation to embarrass him in front of everyone and get him fired, these days that is easier to do. But will it change Ray's behaviour? And will it change the way others behave in the organization?

Now, I know what you're thinking. It is easy for me to write this here. I love an off-the-cuff quip back at my detractors on Twitter. My whole schtick of fearlessness comes from my ability to stand up to racist, sexist bullies with a witty remark. It rarely changes things, but my motivation is always to let others see that it is possible to fight back against bullies, and you don't have to sit in silence and take a load of abuse. I want people to know that accepting viciousness and vitriol is not the new normal. Sometimes the motivation for not being a bystander to a prevailing trend of malice is just to remind people that there is an alternative to taking the bullshit.

But people regularly take wrongdoing against themselves very personally, especially if it is traumatic; it does feel very personal but often it isn't. Making it about *you* rather than about *them* has the effect of making you think that it is an isolated incident and that this hasn't happened to others. Always remember the rule of exceptions: the powerful are constantly trying to turn things into an exception rather than a rule. This is almost never the reality. Zelda Perkins found out after 20 years that she was most certainly not alone in being silenced by a sleazy boss. She was not a terrible exception; her story was part of a trend in major companies, universities and public bodies. It turned out NDAs were and are being used all over the world by wrong 'uns who want to keep their chiefdoms.

Stop yourself before you step forward and ask the simple questions, why am I doing this and will doing this make things better in the long term or allow others to feel empowered to speak up too? If the answer is 'yes', then do it, be brave and bold and brilliant. If the answer is that you want to prove a point, stick in the knife and put two fingers up at the establishment, I would save yourself the bother – the establishment is much fitter for this fight and it will probably crush you.

———

It was only after nearly 20 years, in October 2017, that Zelda Perkins' willingness to speak truth to power finally paid off. When the dam broke on the Weinstein affair, and actresses and women who had worked with Weinstein all stepped forward together, Zelda felt that she could finally break her silence. 'I first told my story publicly to the *Financial Times* a week after the Weinstein story broke. My own lawyers wouldn't let me break the agreement and I couldn't get any other legal advice on it (which made me even more furious and aware that the legal system was protecting Harvey). I urgently wanted to break the agreement publicly to give other "victims" the courage to do the same, as I hoped and believed public opinion would be on my side, even if Harvey or the lawyers wanted to come after me. To be honest, this was the only moment I felt fear.'

Then, in front of the Women and Equalities Select Committee and covered by the laws of parliamentary privilege, a law that protects what is said in parliamentary proceedings from being used in any legal proceedings, Zelda finally got to publicly release the details of the egregious legal documents that had bound her to secrecy and deterred her from speaking to police, medical professionals and anyone else. The most important lesson I think we can learn from her is that against all the odds, all the social markers that when put through any risk assessment would have told her, you tiny dot of a young woman are not going to be able to stand up to this force, she still dug deep and did it.

Zelda was silenced for decades by powerful people, and because of these shackles she was not able to do all the things that would help a person really fight back and make a change. She couldn't find others in her situation, she couldn't beam her story around the world, her NDA said she couldn't even speak to a counsellor about it. Zelda had the courage to stand up and be counted and the powerful knew how dangerous that was so they had to do all they could to shut her down.

Since the dam broke on the Harvey Weinstein

scandal, she and others have freed themselves from their shackles. Zelda has used her voice and courage to work with parliament, the media and lobbying groups so that her experience can finally truly change things. In some states of America now NDAs are banned in cases of sexual abuse and harassment. In the UK the evidence given by Zelda Perkins in our parliament has and will continue to change the regime of NDAs.

Zelda's decision to speak out inspired an entire parliamentary inquiry into the use of NDAs being used by the rich and powerful. When we finally change the law to end harmful silencing practices, which I know we will eventually, it will, in my opinion, be Zelda's law.

———

So, can you speak truth to power? Yes you can.

Taking the first step is just that. You can do it, you don't need to be a superhero to step forward and say, 'Hang on a minute.' Don't ever feel like you must wait for the really bad thing that you think might happen to happen before you do something about it. If you think something is wrong, ask around – other people probably think it's wrong too.

Give yourself permission to ask questions, seek answers and fight back. Don't wait for someone else to do it; they are probably waiting for you. Never ever waste a crisis but be prepared that the crisis alone will not carry you through. In speaking truth to power, this is simply the first step of many you will take.

2

FEEL
THE
FEAR

WHEN I WAS A RATHER precocious teenager, I said to my mother that one day I wanted to win the Nobel Peace Prize for changing the gun laws in America. My mother said to me with absolute certainty, 'They will kill you before you even have a chance to start.' Put aside the fact that the likelihood of a British teenager with literally no links to the US or understanding, then, of their legislature had any chance of achieving such a lofty feat, my mom was right that such a task would put my life at imminent risk.

Fear is often used to control us and curb our liberty.

Fear that we will lose our jobs, our homes and our security will stop us in our tracks no matter how right we are. Fear is the thing that will always make us think twice about speaking up.

Some of the people whose experiences I draw from here made the ultimate sacrifice to speak up. I am not, for one second, suggesting that is something most people would or should ever be expected to do. I hope that through reading their stories you are not only inspired by their courage but also that you can see what we must fear if we don't try to curb dangerous and powerful forces.

SILENCE WILL NOT PROTECT YOU

'Fear, unfortunately, is the greatest enemy of freedom of expression – and of dialogue. Fear leads to the dangerous situation where individuals are gagged, forced to retract what they have said through some form of intimidation, or by some other means discredited … Individuals should never be nailed for exercising the legitimate right to speak their mind.'

These words were written by Daphne Caruana Galizia. Daphne was a Maltese journalist who spent her entire career uncovering the wrongdoing and corruption of the Maltese government. She wrote about the scandal in the selling of Maltese passports by government officials to rich and powerful businessmen from outside the European Union who wished to gain financial access to the EU. Before anyone else, Daphne Caruana Galizia was investigating how her government and others may have been involved in Panamanian tax evasion and off-shore financial corruption. This was eventually uncovered when 11.5 million documents containing personal financial information about wealthy individuals and public officials, showing examples of fraud, tax evasion and evading international sanctions, were leaked to journalists. The story was a global scandal implicating many powerful people and governments – including the UK government. Caruana Galizia was undoubtedly one of those who helped to bring about the revelation of this global scandal.

Throughout her career Daphne suffered several attempts on her life and a constant merry-go-round of legal actions against her because she successfully spoke truth to power. On 16 October 2017 Daphne Caruana Galizia was killed by a bomb that had been planted in her car. She died just metres from her home.

The case of Daphne Caruana Galizia is an extreme example of the risks people take when speaking truth to power. She has become a global totem of courage, but when I met her son Paul to talk to him about the risks his mother took, the thing that struck me more than anything was how ordinary their lives had been. He told me stories of the normal things his mother did, like tending the garden, and spoke about times at the beach with him and his brothers. Paul is a similar age to me and, like me, from a family full of boys. His life with a woman who took on the power was very ordinary; she cooked dinner, packed their lunches, moaned at them about their homework. To him she was just Mom; to us she is a beacon of hope that some people face down the fear and keep going.

'My mother used to say, how could you possibly stay silent against that oppressor? All you have is your voice. She used to say that you know you're taking the side of the oppressor if you keep silent and do nothing. Lots of people tried to stress to her that she was putting her family in danger, that sort of thing, her response was always, "I'm not putting them in danger, you are.'"

Daphne Caruana Galizia knew that she had more to lose by doing nothing. Silence will not protect you against your oppressor; silence will only protect your oppressor.

She knew that while her personal safety may be threatened, if she took the side of the corrupt, in the end that would endanger the future of herself, her children and her country more.

Everybody worries about the consequences to themselves and their families of taking a stand. This is a perfectly normal human reaction and, frankly, those that say they don't worry are lying. When speaking to Paul Caruana Galizia I was struck by how many times he would have been used against her; how her children would react if the worst were to happen, was put to her repeatedly as a mechanism to try to stop her. So, I asked him how he felt the risk she took had affected him. If he had been able to stop her to protect her and himself, would he have done it? 'I would have done things differently, I would have spent more time with her. I wish I'd known just how bad it had got at the time. I wish I had asked her to leave Malta and continue writing from somewhere safe. But not talking was never an option. That would have been a death. Everything you've ever done, and you've believed, just throwing it all away was never an option. So, I wouldn't have stopped her if I could. That's how I knew her, that's who she was. I am really very proud of her.'

I do not tell this story to get you to accept a fatal risk in the pursuit of speaking up; I tell it to try to express that doing nothing will not protect you or your loved ones either. Of course, not everyone is taking on global powers and uncovering illegal financial networks and corruption, but Daphne's words should ring true as much in our everyday lives as in this extreme case.

If you don't fight back when the boss at work abuses you and your colleagues, it will never stop. If we act as bystanders to wrongdoing, eventually the wrongdoing will end up at our own door.

I have my own experience of loss caused by political terror. My dear friend Jo Cox was assassinated by a far-right terrorist because of her willingness to speak up about multicultural communities and the plight of refugees. She was shot and stabbed in the street of her Yorkshire home town while her killer shouted the far-right slogan, 'Britain first'. Like Daphne, Jo was willing to stand up and tell the leaders of her country where they were going wrong. She used her position as a Member of Parliament, who had worked for years in war zones as an aid worker, to criticize the government's response to the 2015 refugee crisis and their response on the ground in the conflict that still rages today in Syria. She felt as if people were looking the other way and forgetting their responsibility. Unlike Daphne, Jo was not murdered because she criticized the government, she died because she spoke up for people beyond our borders.

To say you are willing to die for your cause is using the masculine language of war employed to motivate soldiers on a battlefield; it has little relevance to normal people's lives. Jo and Daphne were both incredibly normal people and if they had been asked if they were willing to die for what they believed in, inevitably both would have thought about their children and loved ones and answered that they were not. But … if they had been asked, 'Are you willing to stop speaking up in case you die because of it?' the answer would have been a resounding, 'No.'

Every single day of my working life people try to threaten me for speaking up. If I speak out against the anti-Semitism in my own political party, people threaten my job. If I speak out against the abuse of women at work or online, people literally threaten to rape me. I have had people threaten to kill me, threaten to kill my children; I have been sent creepy messages from people saying that they are following me. When I visit countries whose regimes I have criticized, it is certain that I will be followed and monitored while I am there. If I report what I have seen when I get back to the UK, it is likely that I will not be able to return so freely to those countries.

The day I left my home to board a train, to go to work and commemorate my friend Jo Cox, my son asked me not to go. He pleaded with me, asking me if it was worth it. The answer I gave was that of course I don't want to die, and I would do whatever I could to protect myself, but that yes, ultimately it was worth it to me. To have the privilege of a public voice like Jo and Daphne, and to have the chance to use that voice to do good is worth so much.

I cannot ask Jo the same question: was it worth it? Because I cannot ask her, I must turn to the words she spoke in parliament for an answer; it was not difficult to find. In May 2016, just a month before she was killed, while speaking in a debate about taking military action to save Syrian lives, Jo said, 'Does the Minister agree that it is time for the leaders of both our countries [the UK and the US], even in the midst of two hotly contested political campaigns, to launch a joint, bold initiative to protect civilians, to get aid to besieged communities and to throw our collective weight behind the fragile peace talks before they fail? I do not believe that either President Obama or the Prime Minister tried to do harm in Syria but, as is said, sometimes all it takes for evil to triumph is for good men to do nothing.'

Jo knew that doing nothing will only ever achieve nothing.

USE THE FEAR LIKE A FORCE

'I would definitely do it again. Actually, I'd do it with more gusto than I did before. When you first start on these journeys, you have no idea you'll end up being followed by private investigators working for Rupert Murdoch. I was very, very frightened for a long time.

'People around me were frightened. People suffered emotionally because of that campaign, people I loved. That all goes with time, you have to end up finding forgiveness, otherwise you just eat yourself. But I would definitely do it again.'

These are the words of my friend and colleague Tom Watson, the Labour MP. Tom found himself on the end of one of the worst campaigns of intimidation I have ever heard about when he started to uncover the scandal that journalists were routinely hacking people's phones to get stories. 'I met a woman, who was described as Ms X, who was a victim of a sexual crime and the alleged abuser was in the public eye, and she came to see me and said, "I feel doubly violated by this. This guy did this to me and then the *News of the World* hacked my phone and my parents' phone and tried to write a story about it." Once someone sits in a room with you like that you can't walk away from that; she didn't have a voice and I did have a voice.'

Tom explained the sort of pressure he faced when he looked into the scandal. 'They commissioned a former Metropolitan Police officer trained in covert surveillance to follow me. The undercover journalist Mazher Mahmood was tasked to go through all my private life. I was libelled on the front page of the *Sun*, accused of being part of a plot to besmirch the characters of families of Tory MPs. It was completely untrue. I subsequently won the case. They exerted political pressure on people in Number 10 Downing Street to try and get me to withdraw the libel case. Then, when I ended up on the committee that was looking into the press, I was followed by private investigators. I was insulted by their editors. They put round rumours that I was an alcoholic who needed to go to the Betty Ford Clinic. They said that I was on a mad vendetta. They denied outright that there was any criminal wrongdoing going on at News International. They used their network of powerful people to talk to me softly, softly, or tell me it wasn't in my interest to keep looking into it. So, essentially, they threatened me. People often presented trying to stop me as kindness, doing me a favour, they were trying to sort out what they thought was a political problem with a very powerful entity. It was very, very lonely. There are people in the public eye who were frightened to be in the same room as me, in case they'd be seen as an associate in the eyes of the News International people, one who ran for the leadership of the Labour Party. There were very close friends who suggested some form of media management, who were desperately worried about it, and suggested I was having some form of nervous breakdown rather than just being very, very upset at illegal activity, and intimidating conduct.'

What Tom realized and still realizes is that if powerful people are scaring you and intimidating you, it probably means that you are on to something. It should be used as an indicator that you should keep going – not that you should stop.

So often when we face initial fear of speaking up we must dig deep and use that fear as the force that drives us. Focus on the clear outcome of what you are trying to do, what you are trying to uncover. Without a proper pathway or idea of what you are aiming for, what good looks like, the fear will inevitably sweep you aside. If you know something can be better, and you can visualize the end and what it would feel like to win, the fear of what you are doing in fact becomes a very powerful force. People say it is the hope that kills you in the end. I'm not sure that is true, but it can lead to a lot of high expectations and disappointment. I have always found that the combination of hope and fear is like rocket fuel to keep me going.

MINIMIZE THE RISK

REDUCING THE RISK to your safety that may be a consequence of standing up for yourself and others is often hard to quantify and advise. Those who have given their lives never could have known what was going to happen; if they had known, they would have put every possible protection in place. Since Jo Cox was murdered, MPs – especially those at most risk, like me and other women – have taken precautions and got in what security measures we can. But ultimately, unless we are willing to lock ourselves away – which is, of course, the aim of those who wish to scare us – there will always be a risk. Don't be cavalier about that, I'm not. I take every single possible precaution to make sure I am safe but not silenced. If you are worried that you are at physical risk, tell someone, seek a second opinion, don't worry about raising a false alarm; false alarms are nothing to be ashamed of, not listening to your gut and getting harmed is considerably worse. You might be making a fuss, but who cares? Make a fuss.

WHAT ARE YOU WILLING TO LOSE?

RECENTLY, just a few roads from where I live, there has been a protest outside a local primary school. The protest is mainly being run by a small group of members of the Muslim community who do not want their children being taught about LGBT families. They have objected to the use of texts in the school that include stories about a baby with two moms, or two male penguins adopting and raising an egg together. They do not think that it is age appropriate to teach children that some people have two mommies or two daddies. The protests have been angry and aggressive, and some protestors have been filmed saying things like, 'Women were created by God for men's pleasure,' and holding up banners saying, 'God created Adam and Eve not Adam and Steve.'

I never expected in my brilliant, peaceful and multi-cultural city to have to face bigoted protests on the street just minutes from my home. The protestors have managed to pressure families into withdrawing their children from school with what I consider to be shameful and bullying tactics, leaning on people's religious belief and cultural shame. On one occasion the school had to close early to keep the staff and children safe from a large planned protest. This protest was not just frightening and bigoted, it was damaging the education of children in my community.

I felt as if I had to do something to stand up to the bullies, so I went to see the head teacher to make a plan about applying for exclusion zones around the school to keep protestors from disrupting the lives of children aged four to eleven. The story was big news, so when I came out of the school there were around ten news cameras. I was filmed taking on the lead protestor, a man who doesn't have children at the school but is rabble-rousing anyway and seemingly enjoying the attention. You might think that in this situation I have the power: I am a Member of Parliament. However, the electorate in my constituency, especially those that vote for my political party and give me my power, are in no small numbers drawn from the Muslim community. Taking on this issue is sensitive and my taking on the protest has far greater risks for me than it does for the protestors. The altercation I had with the chief protestor was very public; it was played on every UK news channel and across social media. Millions of people will have seen me doing it, and once done, this could not be undone. In the clip that went viral, the protestors accused me of intolerance of Islam. For someone in my position in my community, this is a dangerous accusation. It is, of course, false; I just believe that all must be tolerant of each other, you don't get to pick and choose which equality you like and which you don't.

I also felt that the protestors were not representing the Muslim community I grew up with and live side by side with, who are not hateful bigots, and I didn't want them presented that way.

But it was a huge risk to me, as one of the headlines, for example, stated, 'Jess Phillips takes on the Muslim Community'. This will inevitably be used against me. As I walked up to the school on that morning, I knew this was a risk and I worried how it could damage me. I weighed up the consequences and decided what I was willing to lose. I was willing to lose votes, I was willing to have my words twisted against me. I was *not* willing to let my children and my family – some of whom are gay, and some of whom are Muslim – live on streets where bigotry and hatred are normalized. I was not willing to let the protestors triumph unchallenged because it wasn't just about this one school – if the argument had been won by them you can bet your bottom dollar that there would have been another protest outside another school, and another and another, until it is too much to cope with and everyone decides it's probably better if we just pretend that gay people don't exist in our primary schools. Except they do; they are playing in the sand pits, colouring in their books and practising their times tables and they shouldn't be ashamed.

I rang my husband after the altercation had been beamed around the world and said, 'This will be twisted, and my political opponents will use it against me at the next election.' His reply was simple; he said, as he always does in a totally pragmatic Birmingham tone, 'Bab, I'm sure it won't but if you lost your job because of this, then it's not a job you want. If you have to pretend to be something else and ignore shit like this to be popular, then we are doomed.'

Doing the right thing sometimes means losing stuff. It can strain relations, it can cost you your job and sometimes your safety, and feeling fearful about these things is totally normal, but you must weigh up what you are willing to lose by doing it against what you might lose if you don't. Also, remember that shit storms pass, time heals, losses can be recovered.

Nobody would be willing to lose their life, and nobody would actively seek to sacrifice their loved ones to a cause. Nobody should ever be asked to, but hiding from the fear will not protect us. In the case of Daphne Caruana Galizia, had she stayed silent she might still be here, but the forces that killed her would be much more powerful and she knew this. Her son was very clear about this when he said, 'Yes she was scared, she had fear, she had become quite isolated and had stopped going out to the beach and doing the things she loved, but she didn't stop sharing. In a way that's a personality thing, stopping would have been the last thing she should have done. I remember her telling me, "I am just so tired of writing about all these fucking horrible men all the time." But she would never have allowed them to get her to that point that she should stop. She was scared but she carried on and published a piece right before she was killed.'

Daphne's death has inspired a backlash against the

power that killed her, and her family have hopes that it will be the thing that finally changes their country for ever. 'I think things will change. I think it's one of these moments, you know, either our country faces up to a serious problem and changes or the window closes. My father, my brothers and I will keep going. We have generated so much pressure and attention, they cannot now ignore it. The Prime Minister of Malta is legally obliged to hold a public inquiry but has refused, and so we had to file a lawsuit, so now we are suing the Prime Minister, so he will ultimately concede. The European Union have been trying to intervene, they have sent delegations of Members of the European Parliament to Malta to monitor and write reports. Those are all public and really damning. The European Commission and the Justice Commissioner have been vocal on issues that my mother investigated, not just her murder. The public inquiry will allow us, in looking at her murder, to open the question of whether the state failed in its duty to protect. It means we will, as my mother did, open to the public all those failings in the institution. It will be a truth and justice commission and it will be a homage to her work.'

Daphne Caruana Galizia should still be here. Her

family now take on her risks and know that the fear and pressure they face and the risks that they have to mitigate and prepare for are nothing compared to the fear of what would happen in the future if they do nothing.

Tom Watson faced unimaginable pressure and isolation to try to make him stop. But when he weighed up the risks and what he might lose against allowing criminals to hack the phones of victims of abuse, the parents of kidnapped children and, in the very worst case, the phone of the murdered teenager Milly Dowler (which led her family to think that she had listened to her messages and that she was still alive), he decided the risk in doing nothing was far worse.

On 10 July 2011 the *News of the World* printed its final edition. Many of the News International staff and journalists were tried and convicted for their crimes, and the scandal went on to change press regulation in the UK for ever. Tom Watson risked and lost so much in his fight to hold the powerful to account, but the storm passed, he became the Deputy Leader of the Labour Party, mainly on the back of his reputation for being a doughty fighter and a courageous campaigner and, as he said himself, it taught him how to fight harder.

3

WHAT'S THE PLAN?

THE ME TOO movement is a brilliant example of a high-profile moment when people all around the world joined together to call time on bullshit. The hashtag #MeToo was used around the world millions of times. Every single woman I know, myself included, took to social media and told stories of their abuse. 'When I was 11 years old a man pulled up in a car next to me and masturbated so I could see. #MeToo', 'My boss used to ask me to sit on his lap while I went through the morning post. #MeToo', 'When I was 7 my stepdad made me undress for him. #MeToo'.

I imagine it will be decades before we see such a global (albeit mostly Anglophone) example of speaking truth to power. It felt like a tidal wave sweeping across the world. Real change seemed possible, people were losing their jobs, there was a shift in the dynamic where your story and your voice gave you power. Women the world over had had enough and finally the patriarchy seemed to be waking up to the reality of how powerful a collective of women's voices could be.

That's what this book is all about, right? Well, maybe not. Did we make the best of this moment? How much real change have we actually seen?

A few years on, I am less certain that anything beyond piecemeal change has occurred. Yes, Harvey Weinstein denies the charges of rape and sexual assault made against him and, at the time of writing, he is awaiting trial in New York, having paid a million dollars in bail. In some parts of the US, speedy legislators have responded with legal changes to how NDAs can be used – in California, for example, they have been outlawed in cases of sexual harassment and discrimination at work. Progress indeed for the women in California. I am certain that employers across the globe have been given pause for thought about their own harassment policies, and the kind of people who bully and harass at work are maybe a little more cautious. But I saw from where I work in the UK parliament that even with wholesale policy change and the creation of new reporting and monitoring systems, very little has changed. If you are a young intern working for a British politician, you are just as likely to suffer them using their power and patronage to manipulate you as you were before.

In the week that I am writing this, a female MP called me for advice about the possibility of the media exposing how badly her complaint of sexual harassment had been handled. She told me on the phone, 'I just don't want this to be the thing I am known for; this will damage my reputation and I want it to go away.' The man she accused still holds a senior position in parliament. In the UK parliament it was essentially the rule-breakers who got to make the new rules. Every single man I have received disclosures of sexual harassment and abuse about at my workplace is still walking around, voting in the same lobbies as me, sipping tea in the tea room.

As part of the work of the Women and Equalities Select Committee in the UK, of which I am a member, we have published three wide-ranging reports on Sexual Harassment in Schools, Sexual Harassment in the Workplace and Sexual Harassment in Public. To date, almost every single recommendation – such as placing a duty on employers to prevent sexual harassment, to reinstate protection for people sexually harassed by customers or other third parties, or to change the way non-disclosure agreements are used – has been roundly rejected or kicked into the long grass of a government review. I know that with pressure we will succeed in the end, but when trying to shift an enormous cultural power imbalance, it is very tough.

The originators of the #MeToo movement bravely spoke truth to power and the ears of the oppressed sang with the songs of freedom. But without the 'What Next?' planning being coordinated in every single country in the world, without the route map for change from the grass roots up, the songs of freedom always fade to silence.

So how can we make an apparent moment of liberation last? The good news is that there are plenty of things you can do to ensure that real change happens. I spoke to campaigners who have done exactly that, in the hope that we can learn from them.

WHAT DO YOU WANT TO ACHIEVE?

THE FIRST STAGE of any plan to try to change things is to work out what the last stage looks like. What exactly are you trying to achieve? Without specifics you will inevitably be pulled all over the place and the people with power you are trying to stand up to will design an outcome for you and then expect you to be grateful for it. If you complain to your boss that your office hours are unfair, without a clear idea of what would be better, don't be surprised if what is then offered to you is as unhelpful. If you are not happy with the way that the council is ripping up all the trees on your street to put in new street lights, you will simply be ignored unless you have a concrete solution to counter their plans.

Too often people fall into the trap of having a grievance. A grievance is easy to ignore or placate as you would a child by offering them a toy. You and the people you are trying to help must settle on an agreed outcome, otherwise you will make a rallying call that leads to little.

On 14 June 2017 a fire broke out in the 24-storey Grenfell Tower block of flats in North Kensington, West London. As a result, 72 people died in the blaze and more than 70 others were injured; 223 people escaped. In the aftermath of the fire, many of the residents spoke to the media about how the situation on the night of the fire had failed them. Access to the site for the emergency services was limited, and the cladding that had been used to insulate the building spread the fire rather than resisting it. Both issues had been raised by residents in the tower before the blaze. No one had listened.

What happened next is a textbook example of how having a plan and clear aims can lead to long-term change. You might think that in the aftermath of such chaos and horror, the last thing that anyone involved would feel like doing is sit and have a meeting about what they wanted, and yet that is exactly what they did.

In the weeks and months that followed, the surviving victims and the bereaved were forced to campaign to ensure that they were heard. Survivors formed a collective called Grenfell United and have spent the years following the disaster speaking truth to power about safer homes and better social housing, and trying to make sure that the voices of those who live in social homes are heard in decision-making about where they live. In the tragic case of Grenfell Tower, this hadn't happened before the fire. If it had, perhaps fewer people would have died.

I spoke to Natasha Elcock, chair of Grenfell United. On the night of the fire Natasha was asleep in her home on the eleventh floor of Grenfell Tower. She recounted to the Grenfell Tower Inquiry that she, her partner and her six-year-old daughter were trapped in the tower for hours after the blaze started. She used bathwater to put out flames as their flat started to catch fire. Natasha put a plug in the bath and left the taps running, throwing out water onto the spreading flames as she and her family waited for help. She repeatedly rang the emergency services, begging them to help her and her family. She was told to try to make a run for it but every time she tried, the heat on the landings sent her back. The family were rescued almost four hours after the blaze began, when her sister directed fire crews to their flat.

When I went to meet Natasha, she is in the beautifully bright and clean community space created for the families affected by the fire. Brightly covered sofas, games areas, board rooms and a café-style kitchen make it look more like the offices of Google than a place you would associate with such sadness. This was a place of recovery and action and Natasha recounted to me how they got organized.

'When the fire happened, chaos commenced. The fire happened on the Wednesday morning, people were just scattered all over the place. No one had taken control of the situation. But by the Friday we had created the WhatsApp group, so we could talk to each other. We set up in a local community centre and made sure that the doors were strictly only open to survivors and the bereaved, so we weren't being infiltrated. That became our base. Just days later there was a meeting that was held and Grenfell United was formed. It was like, look, no one's coming to help us, we're going to have to help ourselves.'

Natasha went on to tell me about how a few people in the tower were instrumental in setting Grenfell United up and that they not only relied on people who had lived in the tower for years and had a history of campaigning for improvements, but also encouraged younger and newer residents who were willing to take things on to the step up. 'In the meeting of the families just a week after the fire, we elected official reps for a three-month interim, and then we started to meet regularly with all sorts of ministers and politicians.' Within the week, they were holding secret meetings with the UK Prime Minister.

The key to the successful planning of Grenfell United was not simply that they were a group of activated people thrown together in tragedy, it was also how they decided to organize and set clear goals. They had a plan.

'A lot of people kept saying they wanted justice, but we couldn't work out what justice was. Justice, justice, justice; to this day, I still hear people screaming for justice, but I always say, what does that mean? What does justice mean? What we did was to start by asking what survivors wanted and needed. When we had that, we broke it down into short-, medium- and long-term goals. In the short term, we decided, let's get everybody in a house. Let's get everybody settled. We wanted to make sure it was us leading the demands and to stop the government spin. The government were making ridiculous promises that were unrealistic. We knew that. Then our medium-term goal became about getting people to decent mental-health support. Let's get people in a place where their mental health and the health services for their kids is good. Only when that was done did it become about legacy and making sure people who live in estates in social housing are being listened to and able to have a voice to make changes, because we weren't listened to.'

In the two years following the Grenfell Tower disaster there have been plenty of other issues that the families have had to contend with, such as the launching of an official inquiry by the Prime Minister (which was not demanded by Grenfell United). Also, a long obsession in the media and in parliament about the types of fire-resistant cladding on buildings, again not something that Grenfell United have obsessed over. They have, of course, responded as a collective to all of these incidents, but they did not allow these things to derail or distract them from their clear and defined aims. They stuck to their planned goals and focused on creating the outcome they wanted to see. All around them politicians, the media and other campaign groups have had other agendas and narratives, but their planning and the way they organized has allowed them to remain focused.

On the day I met Natasha Elcock, it was almost exactly two years on from the Grenfell Tower fire. All but 12 of the hundreds of families had been rehoused in places of their choosing. Of the 12 still waiting, most were awaiting their homes to be adapted and finished before they could move in. The group had worked with local NHS services to change the process for adults and children accessing mental-health support, not just for them but for others in their borough, too. On the very day I met Natasha, I got home, turned on my computer and I had received hundreds of campaign emails from ordinary citizens all over the UK, demanding that I, as a politician, listen to the Grenfell United families' appeal that the government set up a new housing regulator. The emails, from people who had never met any of the Grenfell families but had joined with them in their organized campaign, read:

> I'm writing to you as I believe the government should create a new housing regulator that works for tenants, not just landlords. People living in social housing should be treated with dignity and respect and concerns should be listened to and addressed.
>
> Almost two years since the fire at Grenfell, we still have a system that too often ignores the concerns of tenants. And while the Grenfell Tower fire was an unparalleled tragedy, up and down the country social tenants know what it's like to have their concerns brushed aside.

Of course, I will support them.

Natasha and her neighbours were successful in taking action not because of guilt about their situation, not even because of the media coverage; these factors helped but alone they wouldn't have worked. Grenfell United wrestled power away from those who harmed them because they had a plan, and that plan had clear and achievable demands.

I cannot count the times I have been expected to be grateful for the simple act of a blatant wrong being put right. I have lead campaigns about funding for women's refuges that had been cut; I have fought for blocks of flats where I live to have heating systems put in place, so residents are not freezing in the winter on a 1960s system that doesn't work; I have gone to the government and made the case that we need services for children and families who have suffered domestic abuse. Each time I have had to push back against what those with the power told me was an acceptable solution. Each time I pushed back with clear demands. Those who hold the cards will often tell you that you don't understand why things can't be done, why something isn't possible; it's a derailing tactic. I have been told by powerful commissioners and government ministers, for example, that I don't understand how women's refuge funding works, and that I am being naïve in my demands. And that is in spite of the fact that I had managed a women's refuge budget, been a local council commissioner for women's refuges and had the full weight of the entire women's sector behind me. I've forgotten more about refuge funding than most of those I go up against will ever bloody know. Often those who are campaigning for justice or to right a wrong are far greater experts on the issue than the powerbrokers they are challenging. Who knows more about living down your street – the man in City Hall or you?

If you have a clear set of reasonable and achievable objectives from the beginning, they will always be your touchstone. Be prepared to seek compromise but don't let the powerful patronize you out of following your vision.

FIGHT THE WAR YOU HAVE NOT THE WAR YOU WANT

I WOULD LOVE to advocate overhauling all our slow global systems to make wholesale change; however, this is an entirely unrealistic and is usually only shouted about by people who do very little to change stuff and just like to whinge. People have become too purist about taking action. As far as I'm concerned, the voices that tell you that you should do nothing until you can change everything should be roundly ignored. They are usually the kind of people who raise six hundred points of order in a meeting and like the sound of their own voices. Leave them to listen to themselves while you crack on.

I have seen first-hand and on social media people criticizing others who are using less plastic to try to save our oceans, telling them it is pointless while China is still largely a coal-powered nation. There is almost nothing the average person can do about the coal consumption of the second largest economy in the world, but it is utterly defeatist to suggest that we cannot take our own small actions. Don't expect the Nobel Peace Prize for moving from plastic to paper straws but also don't give up on trying to do your bit.

Alas, we must fight the war we have, not the war we want, and that means working within the systems that we have in order to change things. I hope that with every change we evolve our global power structures, but let's be realistic about what we as individuals can do, and get on with doing it.

In your life you have more opportunity to use the systems in place to change stuff than you might think. In fact, most people have absolutely no idea of what rights and powers they have to stand up to wrongdoing. At work, more so than anywhere, the policies and procedures are meant to be there to protect you and your bosses equally, but your bosses are often the ones who write those rules. Everyone has pretended in their first few days of a new job to read through all the policies and procedures, which is more of a chore for most than an act of insight.

No matter what the bullshit is that you want to call out, find out about the rules of the institution making the mistake. Big businesses all have boards and shareholders and will be governed by some sort of code of conduct.

In the initial planning stage of any action I would recommend finding out what these rules are so you can plan a line of attack. Find out what institutions are saying that they are doing and use this as a basis to critique practice. Every single company in the world has a mission statement that looks to make grand claims beyond wanting to make profits.

For example, a quick look on Google tells me that the mission statement for taxi firm Uber is:

> **Uber's mission** is to bring transportation –
> for everyone, everywhere. **Vision:** Smarter
> transportation with fewer cars and greater access.
> Transportation that's safer, cheaper, and more
> reliable; transportation that creates more job
> opportunities and higher incomes for drivers.

Now, if I worked at Uber and I had a problem with the way staff and drivers were being treated, or if I as a customer of Uber had a complaint about poor service, or a safety concern, the first thing I would do in making a complaint, either to them or publicly on a social media forum, would be to use the company's own words and point out where it wasn't living up to its own self-imposed standards and values.

In the case of Uber, its commitment to 'higher incomes for drivers' has been tested in the British courts for three years. In July 2016 the Central London Employment Tribunal began hearing a case against Uber based on the testimony of two ex-Uber drivers, James

Farrar and Yaseen Aslam, about their employment status. In the evidence presented in the initial tribunal, Farrar stated that in some months he earned as little as £5 per hour, well below the UK minimum wage, which was £7.20 at the time. Uber claimed in court that it did not have to guarantee minimum wage standards as the drivers (who argue that they work exclusively for Uber) were in fact all self-employed rather than directly employed. In October 2016 the tribunal delivered its verdict: Uber drivers were not self-employed and should be entitled to workers' rights, including the minimum wage. Uber has gone on to appeal this decision, so far unsuccessfully. However, for our purposes, this shows how we can use the words of a company and what it says it stands for to push back on wrongdoing.

State and government departments will similarly publish their mission statements or vision plans for a certain term of office. If you have a niggling feeling that something is wrong, often the best place to start is looking at these and seeing if they hold water. If planning to take on an institution, often you will need to ask questions and find data to make your case. For example, I looked at the mission statement and values of the Missouri State

Attorney's office. Its mission statement claims:

> To protect and advance the interests of the state
> and its citizens through the judicial and legislative
> process and to serve as the People's lawyer, fighting
> for openness and justice, especially for those who
> have no voice.

All sounds legitimate and reasonable. So how exactly are they speaking for people without power and voice?

A bit of research online shows me that in 2015 the *New York Times* undertook a data exercise that found that in 2015 Missouri had 'more than 100 elected prosecutors, all but one was white'. A quick look at the most recent census for the state of Missouri shows me that 'Missouri's minority population has increased from 16 per cent in 2000, to 19 per cent in 2010. Missouri's population by racial breakdown in 2010 was: White = 82.8 per cent; Black or African American = 11.6 per cent'

We can see from the census that the prosecutors of the State Attorney's office (responsible for prosecuting crimes for the state) are unrepresentative of the population. This, of course, proves absolutely nothing but shows how a little bit of research, using some hard-fought-for systems of transparency, have highlighted further possible questions I could ask if I as a citizen felt something wasn't right in this area. For example, it would be perfectly legitimate for me to write to the State Attorney's office and ask what they were doing to ensure that their mission to seek 'justice, especially for those who have no voice' was including the voices of the 11.6 per cent black population in the state.

The same census data I referred to earlier also shows me that in 2010 the Missouri prison population was 56 per cent black/African American; in fact, 78 per cent of the entire prison population was from a minority ethic group, with white people making up only 12 per cent. I might, if I was a citizen of Missouri, at the very least write to the State Attorney's office and ask them to define 'those who have no voice'.

———

The institutions that we use and rely on have published standards and policies that we can use to legitimately question and scrutinize them.

The tool of holding people to account for their words is used in politics all the time. When Theresa May became the UK Prime Minister, in her first speech she talked about how she wanted to challenge the 'burning injustices'. This inevitably came back to haunt her because every single time her government took away the disability benefits of a citizen who was dying of cancer, or wrongly deported Windrush migrants who were legitimate British citizens, the newspaper headline or the attack from opposition politicians would describe it using the phrase, 'burning injustice'.

Doing research into who holds the power in institutions, and what they say they do with that power and what they actually do with it, is the cornerstone to most successful campaign planning. If you think something is wrong, have a look at what the powerful say they are doing and hold them to account for it.

MIND THE GAP

WE ARE GRACED by living in an information age when we can find out who is on the boards of companies, what they are reporting in their annual returns, who our local council or regional politicians are and how we can speak to them. If we want some information that we cannot find, we are perfectly within our rights to ask for it. Looking at the policies and procedures at your workplace will help you see where there are gaps that you could seek to fill. Your work may not have a specific bereavement policy, for example, or a policy on how to help a staff member who is suffering from domestic abuse. We will never know if the powerful are running roughshod over us unless we look at what they say they are doing and what they are missing.

It is often the case that those with power don't even mean to leave gaps. There is often no malice involved but, for example, if everyone on your company's board is a man, it may not have occurred to them that single moms might need different working hours, or that in the case of bereavement it is usually women who do the lion's share of the administration and could maybe do with a week off work without worrying.

I have been an equalities campaigner all my adult life and much of the work I have had to do – either in companies or councils, or with both national and global government organisations – is to identify the data they are *not* collecting by finding the gaps. Very often injustices are hidden in things that weren't recorded properly. For example, in the week I am writing this I have asked, through a public parliamentary question to the Home Office, 'How many women detained for immigration purposes were identified by immigration enforcement as a result of them reporting a crime to the police in (a) 2016, (b) 2017 and (c) 2018?' This question had come about because a woman in my constituency rang me for help from an immigration detention centre where she had been incarcerated after she had rung the police when her husband threatened to kill her. Her immigration status was linked with her remaining with her abusive husband. I know the answer will inevitably be (because it always is): 'We do not collect that data centrally.' Every time I am given this answer, be it about prison data, welfare payment breakdowns or geographical anomalies in funding, it is always the beginning of a campaign to make them start collecting the data, so we can see where the problems are. Don't worry, I got the woman out of the detention centre and her case is one of many I and campaigners have managed to find, which are now being used to take legal action against the government.

Using this technique of looking for what was miss-ing, I have been able to compel the UK government to collect the data on the number of women who requested separate benefit payments from their partners due to domestic abuse. The data proved that hardly any women (figures have revealed that just 20 claimants were in receipt of split payments across the UK – despite almost 1.3 million claimants of Universal Credit) were requesting this and allowed me and other campaigners to demand changes to the UK welfare system, which was clearly not fit for purpose as abused women were not accessing it. The government told us time and again that they had made sure the system accounted for these cases, but only when we forced the data collection were we able to prove what we knew anecdotally – the system didn't work.

If you are embarking on taking on a powerful person, do some research; don't just look for errors, also remember to look for what might be missing.

PEOPLE IN SMART BUILDINGS WEARING FANCY SUITS

DON'T BE COWED by perceived hierarchies. And don't ever let anyone tell you that you don't know best.

Sadly, lots of powerful people think that the reason they are powerful is because they are clever and brilliant and know everything about bloody everything. I have discovered, since becoming a powerful person who hangs out with other powerful people, that there is an almost exact correlation between people who think they know everything and people who know pretty much nothing. They might know some really fancy words, or be able to memorize the name of a piece of law or some baffling-sounding legal jargon, which they will often employ to create a smokescreen, intimating that they are very bloody smart and you shouldn't try to change their mind. If I had a pound for every time I have heard someone cite obscure Victorian-era law to shut down opposition to their view, I would be as rich as the people who do this. Don't be fooled by it, it is fakery.

I have seen how powerful people try to patronize working-class people who try to fight back. I have watched landlords telling tenants that they are wrong about the damp in their property and that it is not a major problem and they just need to open a window. On one occasion, one of my constituents was told that their property had damp and mould on the walls because they were breathing out too much. Which does beg the question, how much breathing out is too much?

Beware of fake science as much as fancy legal speak. I myself have been told by big tech firms such as Twitter and Google that I don't understand how the platforms work and that my complaints about the abuse I receive on those platforms is somehow not the problem I think it is. On one occasion, Twitter told me that there might be a reasonable context for some of the abuse sent to me. The abuse said that I needed a good fucking to fix my teeth! I'm not wholly sure what context is needed for that, and it is certainly against the advice of dentists. I have watched judges in the family courts telling mothers that they don't understand about the domestic abuse they have suffered. I have watched cabinet ministers patronizing families who have lost their loved ones, claiming that while they feel deep sorrow for their loss they don't understand the system and therefore their demands cannot be met.

I attended a gathering of families who had been bereaved, injured or wrongfully imprisoned because of errors and corruption in state organizations. The families had joined forces to seek better legal funding for individuals who find themselves in a legal battle with the rich state. Hundreds gathered in a cramped room in the House of Commons, designed to make you feel small and excluded. Rooms in parliament are decked with wood panelling, dark Victorian wallpaper and portraits of austere-looking men from history. In the room were mothers whose sons had been killed due to how they were restrained in mental-health institutions, families who had never had justice for their loved ones blown up in the bombs of the Irish Troubles, sisters of brothers who died of AIDS because of contaminated blood they were given by the NHS. So often the people who are forced to fight back against a powerful state are those who must rely on it, the working classes of any nation.

What I realized from each person who spoke was that every single member of each campaign group was a leading world expert on their case. These were regular working-class people with no legal training who had become versed in the laws and mechanisms of our justice system through their years of experience. Each person who spoke said, 'I know I'm no lawyer but ...' And in that way they diminished their expertise. Often these families present with passion; they are very angry through years of being ignored as well as their initial trauma. Often in these meetings, a well-dressed minister of state and a civil servant sit at the front and act sympathetically but offer very little back in terms of either meeting the demands of the bereaved and maltreated or even inviting them to be part of making change. These families should be treated like the experts they are; instead, they are too often dismissed as emotional and naïve.

Don't ever let those with less expertise than you tell you that their fancy job title trumps your experience. It is imposter syndrome, nothing else. Don't ever march to the tune of those who want to silence you by joining in with them in your own head. It is their mantra that you don't understand how things work and that you don't belong in their palaces, when in reality it is they who have a deficit of understanding.

No one is more of an expert on your life and experience than you. When you are planning, think big and don't eliminate any of the echelons of power from which you may feel excluded.

The difference between the case of Zelda Perkins, who acted with her gut and had little time or opportunity to take stock and plan, compared with that of Natasha

Elcock and the Grenfell United families, who thought through the structures and planned for the best possible outcome, is clear. In Zelda's case she was left powerless and silenced for years with little hope of making the changes she wanted to see. I do not wish to diminish her courage and her eventual efforts to change the law, but merely to highlight how taking time to plan, to take stock, to do some research and identify the problems and the people who can help you and the people who won't, will pay dividends in achieving lasting change. Courage is vital, but although proper research, planning and probing into the power you are challenging might seem less inspirational on the page or in a TED Talk, without it you may well be ignored, patronized and placated.

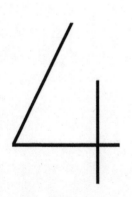

BUILDING MOMENTUM

NO MATTER WHAT your chosen act of resistance is, be it a global campaign or just standing up for yourself against the customer who treats you like crap, having back-up is vital. It's a small thing but every time I fight back against someone being sexist, racist or offensive on Twitter, I know that there will always be at least a handful (sometimes thousands) of others who will back me up. Of course, there are loads of people who use my resistance as another reason to attack me, but within that crowd are other forces of resistance. I know for certain that I wouldn't fight back if all the feedback was going to be negative.

Whenever I have had to dig deep and crush my fear and embarrassment to raise an issue at work about my pay or my conditions, I would always have talked to some trusted colleagues before to make sure that I wasn't being unreasonable or needlessly defensive. When I was a barmaid and some drunk bloke would try to squeeze my arse as I collected glasses, there were times when I knew that there were others around who would back me up if I challenged the customer, even throw him out for his behaviour. In other places I worked where it was considered a part of my job to take sexual assault from customers, I said nothing and pretended I hadn't noticed wandering hands. Back-up matters, if for no other practical reason than it gives people courage.

You do need other people. You cannot do this on your own.

STORYTELLING

OKAY, SO NOW you have a plan, you know your goals and you have a clear objective. The next thing you must have is a compelling case. In order to build momentum beyond the initial shock, incident or discovery of wrong-doing, you will need to tell the story of why something is bullshit.

Storytelling is a powerful tool and too often it is used to spread fear and hatred rather than to activate positive change in our lives. The far right around the world will lean on stories of violence by immigrants to create fear and division.

To rally people to your cause or reach the person whose mind you wish to change, you need to be able to touch them and their lives. Your stories need to be relatable and speak to the humanity of the people you're telling the story to.

In 2018 the whole world seemed to be taking a huge step backwards in the fight for equality and the maintenance of liberal democracy. Middle Eastern countries were ramping up anti-LGBT laws to include the death penalty, US state after US state was lining up to curb the rights of women to make a choice over their own bodies with regressive abortion laws reaching the statute books. Charities offering crisis support in humanitarian zones were being made to stop offering women in the developing world advice on birth control, and anti-immigrant rhetoric was sweeping across Europe in a populist surge not seen since the wars of the 1930s and 1940s. But in one tiny corner of the world, the once conservative and religious Republic of Ireland was leaping forward, thanks to the work of a small group of activists, who hinged their entire campaign on a well-told true story.

Dr Savita Halappanavar died in 2012 at the age of 31 from septicaemia – an infection she contracted because she was denied an abortion during an incomplete miscarriage. Savita Halappanavar became synonymous with the campaign in Ireland to repeal the country's Eighth Amendment that effectively banned abortion in the country. Her story and, more importantly, the image of her face were used again and again throughout the campaign to force a referendum to repeal the law. It was not only the horrific story that caused outrage, but also that the image of this woman's beautiful, hopeful, smiling face pasted on posters across the country allowed the voters in Ireland to see themselves and their own families in her image. If this bright, young, educated woman could be so failed by the system then so too could you, was the message her image sent. This woman could live on your street, you could be married to her, she could be your daughter.

'I still remember where I was when I read about Savita Halappanavar,' recalls Cara Sanquest. Cara is one of the campaigners for the Together for Yes campaign in Ireland and the London-Irish Abortion Rights Campaign in London, who spearheaded the Home to Vote campaign that changed the Irish constitution's draconian abortion laws. 'When we did a debrief session with all of the people who worked on the campaign and in the campaign office, there weren't many people who didn't say that Savita was a factor in bringing them on board. This was a woman who didn't even particularly want to have an abortion. She had wanted a pregnancy that had complications and when she went to the hospital she was failed. The shocking truth is that in almost any other country, she would have been fine, she would have lived. I felt ashamed about the fact that she had come to Ireland as a dentist with her husband, and this would have been their first baby. There was no confusion or complexity in the case, they directly asked, and they were directly told, "You're not going to get an abortion, this is a Catholic country." I think with her story, it was the fact that it could have been anyone who had a pregnancy that had complications, and it just showed how far the reach of the Eighth Amendment of the constitution had got into the healthcare system.' This wasn't about other women who needed abortions, suddenly this story made it about everyone.

Choosing to tell Savita's story changed everything. Even if your campaign seems smaller in scope, you can always find stories that touch people. *This could be you one day* is the vital ingredient in bringing people with you, no matter what the action. You can find ways to show how your hardship makes you feel and try to help others walk in your shoes.

Using the example of your boss picking on you or others at work, the story cannot simply be: *I just don't like it.* It has to be about how it is making you and others feel, and to bring other people along, you need to work to show them how this could just as easily happen to them. If you want to campaign about a business buying up the green spaces in your area to build new high-rise offices, for example, saying *I don't like how it's going to look* makes you appear like a moaning NIMBY (Not in my back yard). If you tell the story of a local youth football team who have always used the green fields to play their league matches and have nowhere else to go, the narrative is no longer about what you do and don't like but about something others can relate to. Going one step further, you could pick one of the children who plays in the sports team who will be losing their pitch and tell the story of why they play, and what it will mean for them to no longer be able to exercise and meet with their friends. You are not only making the campaign about humanity versus the powerful, you are now inviting those you need support from to think of their own lives or the lives of their loved ones. You have connected with them on their terms.

Think this is manipulative? Big business does this all the time. Every bank advert I see on the telly tries to invoke a sense of the customer's life. I am frequently being told I should get my mortgage with this or that company because on their adverts they have a struggling family just like mine, trying to do their best, and the bank is on their side. McDonald's advertise to me and my sons with cute animations about the farmers they use to grow their food, and they show me images of children eating carrot sticks and bags of apples while looking happy with their moms and dads in a McDonald's store. My children have never ordered anything from McDonald's that wasn't a burger, fries and a milkshake, but the technique is used to make me feel less guilty as a mom and reach out to the part of me that cares about my own children's health.

Good storytelling is the catalyst for change in lots of ways but more than anything it is the tool that will bring people out of their homes to help you win your battle.

IF YOU DON'T TELL THE STORY, SOMEONE ELSE WILL

OWNING THE NARRATIVE of your cause and your plight early on will also protect you from some of the techniques used by powerful forces to tell a *different* story. Natasha from Grenfell United talked at length to me about how the narrative of the people who lived in the tower was taken away from the people themselves in the early weeks after the fire. She and the people in her neighbourhood were being presented not as they were but as some down-trodden, impoverished community full of illegal immigrants and the unemployed. The estate where they lived was presented as a forgotten, hopeless wasteland, not a perfectly nice community in one of the nicest parts of the capital. The narrative was formed firstly by some people with good intentions who wanted to highlight the stark difference between the rich and poor, and secondly by less well-meaning forces who wished to 'other' the residents in order to lessen their plight. Each stole the narrative from the actual people involved. Both offered little agency to a group of people who had been so badly wronged and deserved more than ever to have their real-life experiences, both good and bad, heard.

Natasha told me:

'There was a lot of misinformation in the early days after the fire. We've had to try and change the narrative that the block was full of illegal immigrants or that no one worked. It was so far from the truth. We have had to work tirelessly to change that and are still trying to change it. One change I hope Grenfell United achieves is that people will get to see the community that we are. Our block was just a normal block, we are normal people. We're typical Londoners, looking after our families and trying to get by. Yes, some people were on benefits like on any street, but most people go out to work, do what everyone does. Some people wanted to believe we were really downtrodden or helpless. It's important to fight this narrative because we know that other communities are fighting the same problem. We just want to be treated with dignity and respect. We need people to listen to communities like ours to stop another Grenfell, we are just normal people so these attitudes and misperceptions must be challenged.'

The Grenfell families could not control their narrative in the early days; they were busy recovering, grieving and organizing the lives of those who had lost everything. When I sat down with Natasha and other families from Grenfell United, I was surprised by how little I actually knew about the real experiences of the community. I had believed some of the misinformation.

If you do not own the narrative and tell the best and most compelling story early on, you can bet your bottom dollar that the people you are trying to challenge, be it a big, powerful organization or just your boss at work, will paint a very different story. In the case of the narrative that formed about the Grenfell families, it was once again the establishment trying to make an exception of them, to 'other' them and make them not like you but, instead, some sort of Victorian-impoverished urchins, prone to poverty and illegality.

To reach people and rally them to your cause, you must make your story not about how people are different from the norm, but how, like Savita Halappanavar, they are just like you. Don't let the story be about how you or your case is exceptional; remember, this is a tool of control and the story of the everyman or everywoman is much more likely to win you support.

An *it could be you* story is the single most powerful tool you have to rally people to your cause.

WHO'S *COMING* WITH ME?

STARTING SMALL and keeping your expectation ambitious yet realistic will pay dividends when you are beginning a campaign. There are now so many ways we can reach people who might want to join in with us that we can wrongly expect Rome to be built in a day. Cara Sanquest told me how she and her friends at Trinity College Dublin set about starting an activist group to change abortion laws after they were inspired by Savita Halappanavar's story.

'I started a campaign with other friends who were

just so heartbroken after what happened with Savita. First we tried to get our students' union to adopt a pro-choice mandate. It sounds really basic but our college had, in the past, had a head of the students' union who'd been dragged through the courts by an organization called Society for the Protection of Unborn Children, for distributing information about abortion when that was still illegal. So where in the past the college had been active on the issue, because of what had happened in that case, people weren't sure about doing stuff. I and a group of friends basically had to find other people who were angry, so we went out in the middle of the night so no one could see us, and put up posters asking people to meet us and march to the Oireachtas [Irish parliament]. We needed numbers and we knew that if the posters were being put up at Trinity College it would have a certain cachet and would get some attention. Every week, probably for about eight to ten weeks, we did this to take students from the college to a rally and a vigil. I still have the picture of the first week; there were just ten people, but by the end it was hundreds.'

This is an important point: anyone who is going to try to build a campaign about an issue must expect it to build rather than spring up overnight. Social media movements, like we saw in the Arab Spring protests in Egypt and elsewhere, and the images of thousands of women campaigning during the referendum on abortion in Ireland, can give onlookers the impression that on day one, thousands of people took to the streets. This is never the case; there is always a small group of people toiling away in sometimes demoralizing meetings beforehand.

When you are rallying people to action, be pleased if at your first meeting, your first rally or in response to your first declaration on Facebook, only three or four people show interest. Expect no more than 1 per cent return on any marketing, guerrilla or otherwise. In Cara's case, thousands of people will have walked past her posters on the Trinity College Dublin campus and ten people turned up. Too often, people who feel very deeply about a campaign can be easily disheartened when initially only a few people come along for the ride. Three people are better than one; three people can reach three times more new people for the next week. I know it sounds obvious, but I have met many people who gave up after an initially disappointing showing. Don't be disheartened, keep going; change is slow, it takes persistence and disappointment along the way. A critical mass will eventually tip the power in your favour, but a critical mass has to be built.

ASKING FOR IT

IN THE AREA I represent in Birmingham, there is an army of around five hundred volunteers that I can rely on to help me: they will deliver election materials, write testimonials for me, and take out petitions and get them signed by hundreds of others if I need them for a campaign. My army of volunteers are not members of my political party; they are just ordinary people who live in my area. I have been asked in the past to run training sessions on how my team and I managed to build this. I was given a one-hour slot at the Labour Party Conference one year to help train activists in capacity and team-building. It took me three seconds to answer the question, 'How do you activate people to action?' The answer is this simple: 'Ask people to help.' If I were to string this out for ten seconds, I might say, 'Ask people to help, give them something to do and then thank them for doing it.' This is not rocket science but for some reason people are nervous to ask people to do something.

I see thousands of my constituents every year. I help them with their issues, from uncollected bins up to helping them take on legal action against the government. Not all say it, but most who have been helped say things like, 'I don't know how I will ever thank you.' Or, 'If there is ever anything I can do for you, do let me know.' Instead of just accepting their gratitude, I say, 'Well, if I ever need someone to deliver a few leaflets or come and support a protest, can I give you a call?' No one has ever said, 'Absolutely not, how rude of you to ask.' They always say yes.

Think about your everyday life. How often do you ignore the offers of help and support that present as passing platitudes? I bet all the time. People want to help and support each other, but they are often just awaiting instruction. If it is reasonable, I promise you 99 per cent of people will turn up and join in to help if they can. No one will turn up to help with personal or professional tasks unless they are asked to.

Asking people to wade in on an issue is as important

when challenging the small stuff as it is with the big. If you are sick of how one of your mates or work colleagues constantly undermines you or makes your life difficult, but you feel nervous about saying something, ask someone else to do it with you. If you are on the train and there is a bloke being rude and aggressive and you want to say something, ask a fellow passenger if they will back you up. Safety in numbers gives us confidence to speak. If at work you don't like it when customers or clients are rude or aggressive to you, ask your bosses if they will back you up in those circumstances. I wish, when I was 18, I had asked the manager of the bar I worked in if he would back me up every time a customer asked to see my tits. I wish I had asked what kind of support and back-up I could have expected. I wish I'd asked for help.

Asking for help is okay; the worst someone can say is no.

GIVE PEOPLE SOMETHING TO DO

'I DON'T KNOW WHAT, but I just want to do something.' This sentence is said to me more than any other.

Especially in testing times, there are thousands, if not millions, of people in every country in the world who feel hopeless and are looking for direction. Although they could, not everyone is going to front up the resistance like Princess Leia, but there are plenty of people who would be happy to stuff the envelopes or make the tea at resistance base camp. Anyone who has ever run a political campaign will know that there is a job to fit every single campaigner who turns up.

I might be stating the bleedin' obvious here, but this is a huge failing of lots of campaigns. After an initial declaration about wrongdoing, or an initial rally or march, people will ask those involved, 'What can I do to help?' I have written off to campaigners with the same question and at least half the time I get nothing back, or if I do get a response, it doesn't have a clear or defined action for me to take part in. The likelihood that someone who was inspired or activated to join with you at a campaign will stick around for months while you decide on a task for them to do is zero. You may very well have rallied them to your banner, but without clear instructions they will wander off in the crowd, or find some other cause to help.

At the very least, have a universal ask of all who get in touch, such as, sign this petition and get ten other people to sign it in a week, share something on social media, write a letter, come to a meeting, donate some money. Even these small tasks will keep your activists activated until more specific plans can be put in place. This is exactly the same when taking on more personal campaigns. If you are trying to rally your colleagues to campaign on unsocial hours at work, don't just say you are doing it and hope they are with you. Ask them to come to a meeting, ask them to provide evidence, give each person you speak to the task of speaking to at least one other person. Don't look a gift horse in the mouth; turn it into a workhorse.

SPECIALIZATION OF THE WORKFORCE

THE NEXT LEVEL of keeping people motivated is to specialize your supporters. I have turned up to events at my son's school about school-funding cuts and the actions from the meetings have left brilliant graphic designers organizing transport or lawyers making cakes for a fundraising bake sale. A skills audit of the people you have at your disposal will help you target your efforts more effectively. Graphic designers should be tasked with making your media content; lawyers, no matter how good their lemon drizzle cake might be, should be looking at how you might use the law to win.

Specialization matters most when considering who is going to be your best messenger. Even though I have now a relatively powerful public voice, almost every single day of my working life I ask a colleague or friend to say something I think needs saying because, 'it will sound better coming from you'. Sometimes it doesn't seem fair, but in order to be heard you have to find the right voice to get your point across. People are more likely to trust people who are like them, it is one of the reasons that people believe the news and stories shared on Facebook by their friends over news from other sources. Even I am easy to ignore. For example, I have become well known for my feminism, so people can put me in that box and then ignore what I say while rolling their eyes and saying, 'That Jess Phillips, always banging on about women.' So yes, sometimes when we are trying to speak truth to power we need to strategize about those we bring on board to elevate our message. Unfortunately, most powerful people are still men and so sometimes I have to employ the voices of my male allies who will get a hearing. We need to make sure that our voices reach the widest audiences by diversifying those voices.

The London-Irish Abortion Rights Campaign did exactly this. After calling people to an initial protest at the Irish embassy, they needed to keep people involved and organized to turn a rally into the change they wanted to see. Cara explains how. 'I suggested let's have an open meeting, advertise it on Facebook and say that anyone can come. We used the images of our initial protest to inspire people and set up an Eventbrite for people to sign up to and booked a room. Overnight 150 people signed up. At the meeting we invited some people to speak about their campaign experience and inspire people in a big group. Then we split people into groups, and told them that there was no handbook for campaigning to change the constitution in Ireland, it had not been done before, we had to do it ourselves. The groups were 'direct action and protest', 'media', 'fund-raising' and 'political lobbying'. We sent the groups off for half an hour and asked them to come back with a plan in their area and also a completed exercise sheet we had given them of what each of them could do in the next three months, six months, a year. After half an hour we asked them to come back and share their plans and ideas with the group. In those groups they were now in charge of their specialism and each group went on to meet separately about their tasks. They were meeting about once or twice, every one or two weeks. At one point, I would have a meeting every second day after work.'

This is an absolute masterclass in rallying people to your cause, asking them to help, giving them a task and then making it specific and based on their skills. It is no wonder they managed to win a difficult cultural and legal argument in a country where many felt it was lost. I honestly don't know why every political movement in the world hasn't employed one of the women of the Together for Yes or the London-Irish Abortion Campaign to run all of their activism. These women weren't experienced campaigners; they were just ordinary women, students, nurses, teachers, marketing managers.

RALLYING PEOPLE WITH POWER

OFTEN, TO FIGHT a system, we need an ally on the inside of that system, and our political representatives, union officials and civil society reps should straddle both worlds. I understand even as I am writing this that for many parts of the world there is not a well-functioning union movement or civil society and, largely in places where this is the case, the likelihood that your elected representatives are responsive to citizens is slim. In those cases, if you wish to speak truth to power you must try to build these structures. They didn't happen by accident in the places where they exist, they happened through the purpose and drive of activists.

But where these institutions of representation do exist (and so many people have fought long, hard battles to bring these into being), you should make a plan to use them. Of all of the examples I have given about how I have raised an issue or challenged the status quo, very few of them have been about issues in my own life. Most of the times I spoke truth to power was on behalf of someone who had come to me for help as their elected representative on the local council or as a Member of Parliament. Either that or as a member of staff at a charitable lobbying organization. I did not live in the freezing-cold block of flats that leaked water from an ageing heating system. I have never been beaten by my family, left homeless through abuse or ignored by the police. I was never sacked because I didn't turn up to a temp job in high heels, I have never been failed by the family courts system, or been forced to travel for an abortion. All of these are cases where I have challenged powerful institutions entirely because the people involved came to me for help. This is what a representative should do.

If you are planning to start a campaign or fight back against an injustice, you need a plan of who with power and a platform might be able to help you. You should create a hit list of the people with whom you will seek to raise your case. It should be as simple as going to your local politician and asking them for help, but this is where a bit of research on who might be best placed to help you will come in useful. If your issue is a localized one involving your neighbourhood or your employer, your local police force or a problem with the council, then seeking out the help of the local politicians is probably the best way to go. If the problem is your local politician, then (my colleagues won't thank me for this) seek support from their political opposition.

If the issue you are raising has wider implications, even if it is very personal to you – for example, you feel you have been sacked or passed over for promotion because you are disabled – seek out organizations and politicians who have a history of campaigning on such an issue. People contact me from all over the country, and in fact from across the world, on issues to do with domestic and sexual violence because I have a history of raising these issues. Politicians make their names by picking one or two platforms that they campaign on, so there is usually someone somewhere who will cover your issue and may even know something useful about it already.

Do not ever write to all politicians in a group if you expect a response. Every single one of them will assume someone else is responsible for picking it up. The very best way to convince anyone to hear and then take up your case is to ask to see them face to face. Don't be fobbed off by those who are meant to represent you and continue to be persistent but understanding in the face of busy schedules. Offer to go to them.

Don't be afraid to ask them for something directly. Again, just as it is important to plan the outcomes you hope to achieve, it is important to have reasonable demands of those you seek help from. Ask them to write to the people, institutions or government departments that might be at fault. People working for representative organizations are more likely to get answers to questions quicker than you could, so do ask your representatives to ask questions for you. The power of a piece of headed notepaper asking a difficult question makes me want to give every one of my constituents a supply of House of Commons paper. It shouldn't be the case that fancy letterheads open doors faster, but it is, so ask those who have special badges to use them for you.

Be canny and clear about how you ask for help from organizations or individuals. Your burning issue is probably one they have heard over and over again, and while they are often happy to help they are also very likely under-resourced. Have a plan, be direct and ask them to follow up with their action. Go prepared with this and make it as easy as possible for them to help you.

And be nice to their staff, too. I have taken part in campaigns and events because one of my staff has said,

'Please go along and support this man handing in his petition; he was really nice on the phone.'

In fact, if I could have a stand-out piece of advice to anyone trying to rally people to their cause, no matter who it is, it would be: be nice. Be nice even if you are absolutely raging about an injustice because people, even if they agree with you and want to help, find it hard to join in with a person who constantly shouts at them.

And, if you are trying to get politicians on board, don't fall into the trap of political tribalism. You may very well prefer a particular political party – obviously I do, no matter how much they sometimes test my patience – but you have a job to get done, a change to make. If the person who can help you is not from your flavour of politics, you will have to get over that. I cannot count the times that I have sat in private meetings with ministers and politicians from the opposing political party to mine and begged them to change something I know to be wrong. I am willing to give over any credit for changing a law; I am even willing to make my opponents look good if it means I get what I want for the people I represent. I won't pretend it doesn't smart sometimes when I have to watch government ministers line up in front of TV cameras and say, 'Our government will do more than anyone before to fund domestic violence refuges,' when I know full well that they had to be dragged there over hot coals and painful campaigns. The end justifies the means in this instance. Written on the wall in my office in beautiful calligraphy sent to me by a kind stranger is a reminder of my approach to this, it reads: 'I will dance with the devil to make women and children safer.'

I need allies that don't just tribally agree with me to help me speak truth to power. It is fine to have red lines about who you will and won't work with – for example, I try to avoid organizations or people who have been wilfully racist – but don't ever eliminate thoughtlessly some of the voices who could help you based on preconceived ideas. If you are rallying people on your street, put aside the fact that Bob from number 42 is an arsehole who always parks over your drive, because Bob might well be the one who is brilliant at drafting the legal letters you need.

Recently I saw an amazing exchange on Twitter between Ted Cruz, well-known hard-line American Republican conservative and one-time presidential nominee, and Alexandria Ocasio-Cortez, fresh-faced left-wing

Democrat socialist. These two people, who could not ever be considered to be allies, found that they had a common enemy in the big lobbyists in Washington and that together they could potentially be a powerful combo to change the law. Here's how the exchange went:

Ted Cruz:
Here's something I don't say often: on this point, I AGREE with @AOC. Indeed, I have long called for a LIFETIME BAN on former Members of Congress becoming lobbyists. The Swamp would hate it, but perhaps a chance for some bipartisan cooperation?

Alexandria Ocasio-Cortez:
@tedcruz if you're serious about a clean bill, then I'm down.
Let's make a deal.
If we can agree on a bill with no partisan snuck-in clauses, no poison pills, etc – just a straight, clean ban on members of Congress becoming paid lobbyists – then I'll co-lead the bill with you.

When rallying people to your cause you may have to stretch your imagination on who that might be and how they might help. Be open-minded about your allies; as long as you retain a clear goal and an unbending outcome, you will be surprised sometimes by who can help you get it.

5

THE BACKLASH

'I WAS ON TOP OF MY GAME. I thought I was really good at it … And I thought we had the best team. They were really good … really skilled … And to be told we don't want you any more, we don't need you any more … That's quite difficult.'

Sara Rowbotham's words, as she spoke in a BBC interview, bely the pain that she clearly felt from being frozen out of the work she was doing uncovering child sexual exploitation in Rochdale.

But this was the backlash. And a backlash usually means you have hit a nerve.

It can be very distressing, but you can learn to prepare for the worst and harness the power of this, the most difficult part of speaking truth to power to further your cause. Accepting that people will not like you, that they will criticize and lie about you, is something only the very self-assured find easy. For everyone else, it is hard not to let it bounce you off track.

There are many ways in which those who speak truth to power will face a backlash. There are the obvious ways we have already discussed: you can be threatened with losing your job or with legal action. In extreme examples, your safety can be threatened. More likely, it might be said that you are getting a reputation for being a pain in the arse.

However, there are also much subtler and more nuanced attempts to silence, which people are often less aware of, attempts to derail, neuter and indirectly punish you that you won't see coming. We must be prepared for these – and we will hear more of Sara's story later. Seeing them for what they are will help you to move past them and persist.

DON'T SANITIZE

ONE OF THE MOST annoying ways that I feel the backlash when I am enraged and taking action is when people try to sanitize it and water down your aims. This is usually with what seem like helpful little suggestions about how you are doing something wrong, or presents as people trying to push you to go further and take on an even bigger task in the hope that you realize it's impossible and then eventually give up. It can be tricky to tell the genuine from the malicious attempts to stop you.

Remember that you have got to have a clear idea of the outcome you are seeking and keep this as your touchstone. Along the way, in your pursuit of better, people will offer you a lesser solution and expect you to be grateful, tell you a million small reasons why what you are aiming for is impossible and why you should change direction, or they will diminish your efforts as too minor.

For example, let's say a big supermarket is going to open in your area, next door to your children's school. The lorries will be delivering the food throughout the morning each day and this is going to make the road outside the school unsafe for the pupils. You have decided to run a campaign to challenge this and you want assurances that no deliveries will take place between the hours of 8am and 9.30am, ensuring that the streets will be safe at the times the children are going to school. This is a clear and direct outcome you are seeking.

Bear in mind that the supermarket will have staff, planning consultants, lawyers and lobbyists who have been offering all sorts to the local council to allow this to happen. You have got together with parents at the school, you've run a campaign, collected signatures on a petition, and complained to your local councillors and politicians. Your demands are clear. I guarantee you that in this case the following will happen:

The Lesser Solution – The supermarket will offer you a trial run of your demands for a three-month period and a subsequent three-month period where the lorries can come and go at those times. The company will then undertake a thorough assessment of the situation, with you involved of course, and a review will be done. They will report on the review and will decide on a suitable solution six months after the supermarket has been open. This is can-kicking – it seems reasonable but pushes you back a few months in the hope everyone forgets. It is usually combined with offering some sweetener, such as the company will tarmac the playground of the school or buy some sports equipment. This is the nice-guy approach. It is designed to offer you something and then call you unreasonable when you won't compromise.

A Million Small Reasons – You will be told in minute detail the freight and logistics planning for the supermarket chain, which includes huge amounts of data about other stores along the route. You will be told that you are inevitably going to push the problem elsewhere along the line, and then you (not the bloody company who is actually responsible) will be to blame for a blight on another school on another road. You will be made out to be selfish by the million small reasons. You will then be offered the best they can possibly do because of these million reasons that you are too precious to understand and say we could manage 8.45–9.30am.

Too Minor – This is as inevitable as night following day. One of the parents at the school who is involved in the campaign will say that your efforts are not going far enough, that you should be trying to stop the opening of the supermarket altogether. Believe me when I say that this person, while they might not be the most powerful person in the room, is often the biggest barrier to action being taken. Please, dear reader, ignore this person; this person never does a sodding thing to actually change anything but is a horrible distraction and usually the person who will quibble over the minutes of meetings or where the paperclip goes on the petition. This person has as much chance of stopping the supermarket from opening as I have of becoming the Queen of England. Ignore them and feel free to tell them to do one. The supermarket loves this person, the supermarket will negotiate with this person; this person makes your campaign look mad and unreasonable. This person is a gift to the supermarket.

I have seen every single one of these tactics used to try to shut down good people trying to change things. Recently an 'adult entertainment venue' – or, as normal people say, a strip club – has applied to open up in my constituency. It is in a very prominent and visible position on a main road and is near nurseries and schools. Hundreds of residents have objected to it on various grounds, including fear of exploitation of the women who will work there, the proposed opening hours and the noise it will cause, and its basic inappropriateness in the area. My favourite objection came from a woman who told me

I had to 'stop that bloody laptop dancing club', which made me imagine businessmen dancing with laptops. When we made our objections to the council, the fancy agency employed to help the club get a licence came back to us acting all reasonable and understanding and offering us slightly different opening times and noise protections. As if telling us they would open for an hour or so less would now make us all thrilled at the prospect of a huge strip club outside the local school. We were not thrilled!

Be wary of people trying to sanitize your demands or distracting you with talk of a 'bigger picture' or better vision. Stick to your guns and be guided by the outcome you wish to see. Take the advice from a person who has fallen for every one of these tactics. They will all be employed by people, companies and organizations who have been in way more battles than you and know exactly how to play the game.

PLAN THE ANGLES

ONE OF THE SUBTLEST forms of backlash doesn't feel like backlash at all. It is more like pushback. It is often about the details of what you are saying and is a subtle way of suggesting that the challenged understands the situation better than the challenger.

The best way to deal with this pushback is to plan for it. Put yourself in the shoes of the power you wish to challenge and think of all the ways that they may attempt to silence you. Before I take on any battle I sit down with a pen and paper and write down all the inevitable opposing arguments. This allows me to formulate a rebuttal and, in some cases, a detailed and evidenced counter proposal to those arguments when they arise. Also, I would be lying if I said it didn't make me smile wryly at how obvious my opponent is. Power is often quite predictable. The fact that I could almost guess the rebuttals makes me feel as if I am fit to challenge it. The deep and frankly quite smug joy of being able to say to someone, 'Well, funnily enough I knew you would say that and so here is the evidence to disprove your assertions,' always rallies me in a fight.

You should be prepared for the answer you are going to get before you ask the question. In politics, in fact, I have found that the best tactic to head off any initial backlash is to lead with the thing you know the powerful will say and discredit it before they even get to say it.

On one occasion in Prime Minister's Questions, I wished to put pressure on the then Prime Minister David Cameron to change the government's proposal for the funding of women's domestic abuse refuges. I knew that their proposal would be devastating for the women's sector and would cost victims their lives. Saying this to the Prime Minister, of course, should have been enough to convince him of the error. However, I knew that he would have prepared (knowing I was on the list to question him) a stock response about how much the government cared about this issue and that they had shown this by their 40-million-pound investment (a drop in a wide and roaring ocean) in domestic abuse services. He knew I would raise the issue with him, and I knew what his response would be, so I took it away from him by saying it myself. I said, 'Already in 2016, at least 46 women have been murdered in the UK. This number would be much higher if not for specialist refuges. I am standing to beg the Prime Minister to exempt refuge accommodation from the changes to housing benefit beyond 2017. This will certainly close services. I do not want to hear a stock answer about the 40 million pounds over the next four years. He knows, and I know, that that will not stop refuges shutting. Will he exempt refuges? Will he choose to save lives – please?'

My heading off his rebuttal at the pass, meant the Prime Minister was left with nowhere to go but to agree with me, which he did, promising to act on my concerns. Had I not said his argument before he had a chance to say it to me, it is certainly the answer he would have given. If he had been able to use his prepared argument, the effect would have been that he got to patronize me and make out that I was wrong to suggest he was not doing enough. Frankly, he should have judged me as a smarter opponent, but the powerful can be very complacent; we can prepare for this and beat it.

Reader, I won! In 2017 the UK government permanently exempted refuge accommodation from the changes to housing benefit.

Planning for responses like this, and feeling that you have either a solution or a single-line comeback to deal with them, will help you win arguments and also help you not to be pushed off track.

HOW THEY WILL DISCREDIT YOU

BE WARNED – they will try to find a way to discredit your voice. This is very pernicious and can feel incredibly personal, so you need to be prepared for when this happens, and be able to identify it for what it is. If you can do that, you will protect yourself on a very personal level.

The good news is that if the powers that be are trying hard to discredit you, you know you are starting to win. Always remember that power will do anything to survive and its tactics get especially dirty when it feels it is losing control.

The way you will be discredited will usually have nothing to do with the thing you are talking about. Something completely separate will be picked on to make people doubt your voice. For example, I have met women who have made complaints about sexual harassment at their workplace and have found themselves suddenly in a review about their timekeeping or sickness record.

Discrediting is meant to be a distraction, a thing that will knock you off course and upset you. It is often ridiculous and farfetched but that doesn't matter because it is being used as a distraction. Look, for example, at how the US Republican Party tried to discredit Alexandria Ocasio-Cortez when they realized she was cutting through. They released a video of her dancing on a roof from before she had been elected to Congress. The suggestion was that she was not fit for office because in their mind her behaviour was not statesmanlike. It was a weak-ass attempt because frankly she had pretty good moves. It made most people like her more. Similarly, the ridiculous right-wing gas-guzzling press in the UK tried to discredit Greta Thunberg, the 16-year-old Swedish Nobel-nominated climate activist, by writing about how her mom had represented Sweden in the Eurovision Song Contest, like that has anything to do with anything. Again, it backfired and made me personally think that Greta Thunberg was even cooler: I wish my mom had been in the Eurovision Song Contest.

Discrediting the person who speaks up is not, however, always a silly distraction tactic, it can be very sinister and extremely damaging.

———

Sara Rowbotham worked for ten years as an NHS sexual health worker in the English town of Rochdale. It was there that she uncovered evidence of a pattern of horrific sex abuse being perpetrated against dozens of girls by older Asian men. While leading the local NHS crisis team over six years from 2005 to 2011, Sara made 181 referrals detailing the abuse and sexual grooming of young people. Her requests for police and social services action to help these girls, and look in to the patterns of their cases were ignored time and time and time again.

Sara was determined to get those responsible for safeguarding children in the area to listen to her and help her to do something about the hundreds of girls she had come across who were being raped and pimped out by criminal gangs of men.

The cases in Rochdale and Rotherham in the early part of the 2000s have shown how institutional prejudices and excessive caution about community cohesion in fact failed hundreds of vulnerable girls. When Sara started to raise the cases she was seeing with her bosses, she found that the more she pushed, the more her bosses made out that *she* was actually the problem. To protect themselves and to stop their failings being uncovered, they moved to discredit her voice.

Sara told me how social workers and bosses in the

police and the council did this long before she ever spoke out publicly; it started even at the point that she had tried to get them to admit that the abuse was going on. 'It didn't happen overnight. When I started to make more noise and to push them to do something, it took a long time of me shouting and not being heard before being even invited to the meetings. What happened, though, was that they started to describe me as being hard to work with. They said that I didn't understand their processes, and it was me not understanding the job not that they were doing something wrong. One of the social workers asked me if I wanted to take the girls home with me, as if it was me being too emotional and naïve. It wasn't the point, but they tried to make out that somehow it was something to do with me. I don't think I was presenting like that, like some mother earth who wants to rescue everyone, I was a professional woman. They were dismissive of what I was saying and of me. I was saying one thing and they were hearing and saying another. It was a bit like I was seeing salt and they were insisting it was sugar.'

What Sara describes is classic 'gaslighting' – a technique used to make the person speaking up feel as if they might have got it wrong. (The phrase is taken from the 1938 Patrick Hamilton play *Gaslight*, in which a husband manipulates his wife into believing that she is imagining the dimming of the light in their house, while in reality he is causing it by turning on lights in the secretly sealed-off attic). Gaslighting is incredibly powerful and relies on existing hierarchical lines, which breed imposter syndrome. Where seniority trumps experience in our workplaces, this is a technique that is easy to deploy and is usually successful in stopping people who raise issues at the first stage.

In Sara's case, she was the person on the front line in Rochdale and knew what was happening more than her bosses. Don't let hierarchy cloud your intentions or brush your concerns aside.

Look out for the initial brush-off and prepare for it; what comes next is usually worse. If the brush-off and pulling rank fail, those you are trying to call out will next move on to discrediting your character in other ways. I have faced this many times when I have spoken up about racism within my own political party, or its treatment of women, or if I have criticized the government about a specific issue. Those with power and their supporters must try to stop people listening to me, and they will attempt to make me out to be an untrustworthy source. This usually goes from the sublime to the ridiculous. I have had people question my work history and suggest that I don't really have the experience I said I had. I have had my perfectly legitimate office expenses pored over and people trying to suggest I am on the take for having staff and an office, therefore I am untrustworthy. I have had my upbringing and family background questioned, which on one occasion led to my father writing a public response to counter the nonsense. While it was utterly charming, if a little embarrassing, that my 76-year-old dad rocked up to have a pop at the bullies, it shows how when they seek to discredit you, it can reach very personal parts of your life. The fact that I dare to write books is frequently used by those wanting to discredit me, because, of course, I should spend every waking minute of every day being the absolutely perfect representative. So you, dear reader, are now part of the conspiracy, merely by reading these words!

This may all sound like the rough-and-tumble of politics, but it happens everywhere, especially at work, and it happens to normal people who speak up. So, it is really worth preparing for. For example, always keep records of any conversations you have, and keep a note of what, when and how things unfold.

The most common thing I have seen thrown at people who try to whistle-blow or speak up is their sickness and timekeeping are called in to question. Another angle is their attitude to work, making out, as happened with Sara in Rochdale, that they are difficult to work with. 'Aggressive' is a common label for people who talk back. Your qualification for a job you may have been doing for years will undoubtedly be disputed.

One of the most pernicious tactics when seeking to discredit someone is to incite them to behave in an unprofessional way. If you are ignored and belittled you will probably find yourself getting frustrated and angry. If things get difficult you may start to take time off work or stop turning up to events and social gatherings where your aggressors may be. These natural reactions will then be used against you. Friends will start to speculate that you are withdrawn, grumpy or difficult. The fact that you have become unreliable or obsessive will be a mark against you. This is a self-fulfilling prophecy, and believe me when I say that it definitely is used by powerful people fighting back against people who speak up; it is designed to make you question yourself and blame yourself.

———

'I still can't help but think that it was my fault in the way I approached it. If I had been more placid, or if I hadn't lost my temper. I really tried not to lose my temper, but fucking children were being raped every day. I don't know how I was supposed to behave. I'd known these kids since they were 13. There was an arrogance and a superiority coming back at me, like I was dim. I do worry that this was that thing I did wrong. If I'd been more compliant or less volatile, would that have been the key? That was what they said about me in the serious case review, that I was difficult to work with.'

I'm sitting in Sara Rowbotham's little living room when she says these words to me, in her broad northern working-class accent. Her house on a Rochdale street is littered with books and pictures of her parents campaigning. Pinned to the walls are postcards emblazoned with inspirational reminders such as, 'In the struggle between the powerful and the powerless, to do nothing is not to be neutral, but to side with the powerful.' It is very on-brand, and yet even in this temple of righteousness she is still blaming herself. I want to shake her by the shoulders and shout in her face that it wasn't her fault that they wouldn't listen. She still doubts herself for the fact that the police, the social services and all the other people who should have cared didn't listen. I want to tell her that she could have started every single referral with the words, 'Why don't you fucking listen to me?' before detailing the cases she wanted them to look into, and still it wouldn't have been her who was the difficult one. Even this woman, who has now finally been recognized with national awards, whose evidence has seen nine separate trials putting scores of predators behind bars, whose bravery and commitment has been portrayed by Maxine Peake in the BAFTA-winning drama *Three Girls* (2017) is still crushed enough by the experience to doubt herself. Deeply ironically, Sara has been groomed to think this.

The good news is that you can prepare for this. If you know what is happening before or when it is happening, you can see it for what it is – a power grab. With Sara, they tried every trick in the book to discredit her, because it protected them from being discredited. But remember that in the end she still won.

'When I gave evidence on what had been going on to the Home Affairs Select Committee in parliament, I described myself as a social worker and instantly a letter went from the safeguarding children's board at Rochdale Council to the solicitor at my organization, demanding that I prove my qualifications. They wanted to see the certificates, as if I was lying. They were trying to discredit me. Then, because in my evidence I had said that I had made 118 referrals that were ignored, the council wanted me to prove that. We had five police officers come in to go through all our case files to look at the number of times I had made a referral.'

I just want you to let that sink in. When Sara spoke up publicly in the House of Commons, within a few days the safeguarding children's board and the police were poring over her claims, trying to find fault with what she had said. They wanted to make her out to be a liar. The people who had messed up had to discredit the person who blew the whistle. If only they had reacted the same way and shown such determination and vigilance each time Sara had told them a story about a girl who was being sexually abused. When reputations matter more than children being abused, this is the bullshit we must call out.

It was in the end an issue of sickness and absence that was used against Sara by those who could not forgive or tolerate that she had blown the whistle on what had been going on in Rochdale and how it had been ignored.

After the initial court case about the sexual exploitation of five girls, Sara's bosses agreed for her to do an interview with *The Times* newspaper; however, the caveat was that she had to say all was now well and that everything was fine. Reeling from the fact that the police and agencies were still refusing to look into scores of other cases that Sara had identified while she had been working at the sexual health clinic, she refused to toe the line. 'This was my chance to legitimately speak to the papers, so I did. I grassed them up and they did a big exposé on what was happening.' When I asked her what gave her the courage to disobey her bosses and ignore their instruction, she told me, 'I had lost it by then, I was properly outraged, and I'd gone past a point. It was humiliating and demeaning to be told by someone who knew fuck all about my service what to do. I'd been teetering on really poor mental health, all of us in the team had, we feared stepping out of line or standing out, so I just lost it and told *The Times* everything.'

After the interview, Sara lost her job. 'They added up how much sick leave I had had over a two-year period and said if I was to go off sick again, then I was unfit for work. And I did go off sick and in that time the organization went through a structural change. HR and my immediate boss turned up at my house and said that my sick note ran out in two weeks and after that they were making me redundant.'

It is rare that you will be fired or disciplined for seeking justice or doing the right thing, but that doesn't mean that the powerful won't come for you a different way.

Discrediting a truth speaker is a classic tactic, but we can prepare for it. My best advice is to try to guess what tactic they will use, so you can spot it when they do. Keep records and files of all conversations in a work environment and make sure you stick to the rules. I cannot count the times I have had to stop my constituents taking the law into their own hands after weeks of frustration about a drug-dealing neighbour who never gets caught or a dumped car in the street that they have wanted to shift for months but no one listens. Don't do things that will allow people to ignore you further, no matter how much you want to. Right is might and, in the end, it usually will protect you, but don't fall into the trap of allowing them to paint you as being unreasonable and aggressive.

Speaking truth to power is often draining and emotional, but remaining as measured and as reasonable and as professional as possible will not hand them a win. You will inevitably want to howl at the moon and rant and rage when you get frustrated; don't beat yourself up if you do, but bear in mind that it might help the powerful and they might even be driving you to it. Don't let them discredit you, and if they try to with lies and smears, see them for what they are and keep going.

FALLING DOWN THE RABBIT HOLE

I GET A LOT of flack for standing up for what I believe. If I speak up about an issue of anti-Semitism in my own political party, I will for at least three days afterwards suffer a mass of people emailing me, calling my office or sending messages on Facebook and Twitter telling me I am a liar and I am in the pay of the Israeli government, or that I am being paid by some shadowy Zionist lobby. If I speak out about a feminist issue – for example, when

I launched a campaign called #Notthejob to combat sexual harassment and abuse by customers of women working in retail and hospitality – I will receive tonnes of messages about being a feminazi and lies about how I am making up my own experiences of harassment and abuse when I was a bar tender and waitress. Usually when it is anti-feminist abuse it is not too long before it turns to comments about my body and how fat it might be, and there's always a lot of chatter about my tits, which hilariously makes my point for me. I have become well known because I fight back. I pick a few choice examples of this abuse and make them public on social media, coupled with a witty fuck-you riposte. I do it so people feel as if we can fight back. I wasn't always so bold or so able to deal with this backlash. The first time I was subject to this torrent of abuse I tried to fight each and every message and monitor every word. This was a huge mistake.

You cannot fight back against all the people who might criticize you, especially if you choose to use social media as your platform for campaigning. It is too big a task and it is also a tiring and demoralizing waste of time. What I found was happening to me was that I spent so much time fighting back that it stopped me focusing on what I was trying to change and, worse than that, the next time I went to speak up on an issue I had second thoughts about doing it, because I didn't think I had the energy to battle against the backlash. Fighting that backlash made me less likely to speak up. It made me temper my language and actions in such a way as to try to triangulate and avoid the hate; it watered down my voice and weakened the clarity of what I was saying.

———

It is an epiphany when you realize that you cannot please those people and no matter what you say they will slag you off. I kid you not, I can post a picture on Twitter of what I am having for my breakfast and at least 20 people will somehow make a picture of a boiled egg about how fat and ugly I am, the Israeli–Palestine conflict, Brexit and the end of freedom of speech. A boiled egg! My husband once wisely told me, 'Those people hate you anyway; don't worry about pleasing them, instead really give them something to hate.' Following this advice has meant that my voice has remained clear, authentic and believable, rather than mealy-mouthed and cautious.

This is not just a virtual online phenomenon of a feral world, it happens in real life too. People will criticize you for what you are trying to do: at work people will tell you that you are making trouble for everyone, at home or in your neighbourhood you'll get comments like, 'I think you have gone too far,' or 'You're becoming obsessive about this,' and others around those in power or influenced by them will say and do all of the things we've gone over – lies and insults. Don't get distracted with lots of small fights with other people; stay focused on what you are trying to change and the people who can change it. If you end up in a war with the people who cannot help you, you may well put off the people who can by making it look like a huge unedifying battle.

Be strategic about what you fight back against, don't fall down the rabbit hole of challenging it all. Those who don't like what you are saying are shouting at you to try to stop you; don't dance to their tune, no matter how tempting. You will fantasize about the witty replies you could say and play over in your head the smack-downs, but it is all ultimately a distraction. A good tip in this case is to go out with your mates for a drink and indulge in slagging the naysayers off behind their backs. This might not seem like very principled advice, but if it helps you let off steam in a way that doesn't compromise your campaign it will be well worth it!

The Rochdale and Rotherham sexual exploitation scandals changed the way that children are protected in the UK. Every single police force and local authority in the country now has specialist protocols and units to identify, protect and prosecute these crimes. From 2020 it will be compulsory for every schoolchild in the UK to learn about the dangers of grooming gangs and peer-on-peer sexual abuse of children. In the long run, thousands of children will be protected. None of this would have happened had it not been for the bravery of whistle-blowers and the victims who came forward. Sara faced horrendous backlash in her pursuit to speak truth to power; she was discredited and belittled, but she and others changed things. When I asked her if she would do it all over again, she gave me a resounding, 'Yes!' Sara continues to fight every day to improve services for vulnerable people in her town. She is now the deputy leader of the local council. Far from being discredited, for those of us who work with vulnerable girls who have been sexually abused, Sara is recognized as being one of the women who broke the dam.

USE THE BACKLASH

AND NOW HERE'S MORE good news. You can use the backlash as your own force. The backlash is initially scary but in fact it can be a tool. It often proves your point better than you can. A cover-up is often more damaging than the initial wrongdoing.

Being strategic about what you reveal about how the process is trying to silence you will help you to rally support and attention and often is the undoing of oppressors. In the case of those who blew the whistle about the Rochdale sexual exploitation, it was not the revelations about the grooming or the rapes themselves that lead to national policy shifts or changes in practice to help protect vulnerable girls and lock up violent perpetrators. What did that were the revelations about how it had been covered up, about how those who tried to speak up were pushed back, belittled and punished.

I was part of a campaign to try to make women safe on the internet from violent threats of rape and abuse, which I myself have faced. The backlash to that particular campaign was that I was targeted by a prominent alt-right vlogger who started a meme about how he 'wouldn't even rape me', which his followers joined in with, repeating over and over all the ways they wouldn't rape me. This persisted for three years. I am not good enough for a raping; raping is what we do to the women we like, is what is suggested by his comment. Pretty grim stuff. Years after the original slew of abuse that I suffered because of this man and his followers, he ended up standing in an election for the right-wing political party UKIP in the European elections. This had the effect of bringing back to the surface all his hatred for me and started it up again with an even bigger national news platform.

When I decided to fight back against the alt-right abuse I was suffering, it was the fact that I could highlight the backlash I was facing that made my point for me. I regularly use the backlash against me to highlight the original issue I was raising. For example, when this was happening I retweeted some of the worst messages that people were sending me about this 'non-rape' 'satire' so others could see what I was up against. And I tweeted things like, 'Also the rape bit of the non-satire is important, because essentially they are saying that I am too awful to have sex with. Which is objectification, of course, but lads it's not on offer and my husband is well fit.' If I am calling out sexism, I highlight the messages that are overly sexist. I shine a light on what I face when I speak up and without fail it rallies more people to my cause.

George Galloway, a left-winger with a chip on his shoulder, tried to have a pop at me by saying, 'Jess Phillips says I'm a "misogynist and a racist". You see how insane this has all got? Maybe she should consult my Indonesian wife on both counts.' I replied, 'Famously all of those with wives have always been 100% to us gals. Stand down feminists, no need to battle any more.' He also once said that I was 'Sordid, unseemly & grotesque', so I updated my Twitter profile. It still to this day reads, 'Labour MP for Birmingham Yardley. Sordid, Unseemly & Grotesque according to a little man on the internet.'

When I fight back, letters and messages of support will flood in and people offer to help in my campaigns, or even better start new ones themselves. A hundred thousand people signed a petition in a week to bar anyone who had used rape as a threat or weapon online from standing in election. The campaign was started by the Fawcett Society, a feminist organization that felt compelled to action seeing what I and other political women had to face.

Sometimes the hatred and backlash those who speak up face is the thing that causes the change that they want to see. When Brendan Cox stood in the court room on the day the far-right terrorist who had assassinated his wife, MP Jo Cox, was sentenced, he said, 'The killing of Jo was in my view a political act, an act of terrorism, but in the history of such acts it was perhaps the most incompetent and self-defeating. An act driven by hatred, which instead has created an outpouring of love. An act designed to drive communities apart, which has instead pulled them together. An act designed to silence a voice, which instead has allowed millions of others to hear it.'

The backlash we suffer is often painful and personal and it is designed to drive us off track, to distract us and scare us and make us give up. But very often it is the thing that proves our point. It can be terrifying and tiring and you should expect it and prepare for it, but it also is a force we can use for good if we learn what to amplify and what to ignore.

ATTENTION SEEKER

WE LIVE TODAY in a new age of media. Everybody can be a citizen journalist, and everyone can tell their story online and reach an audience of millions within minutes. Social media for all its ills – and they are plentiful – allows ordinary people to share voices and spread causes and compelling video content around the world. It has caused the single biggest shift in power in my lifetime. I sometimes wonder why any company would bother having a social media presence because almost every company you look up on Facebook and Twitter has simply created a space for customers to publicly slag it off. Where once I would have bitched and moaned in an email that I probably would have never even got around to writing to Virgin Trains, when they dick me around on my commute home, now I just get to shame them publicly within seconds of a corporate failing. Powerful people and companies fear social media and how quickly reputations can be dashed, so it can undoubtedly be used in the fight to speak truth to power.

Social media spreads a story like wildfire and can be effectively used to highlight exactly what is going wrong in the world. The powerful image of the bloodied and bruised faces of a lesbian couple, beaten up on a bus in London because they refused to kiss for the sexual entertainment of a gang of young male passengers, travelled around the world in minutes. This allowed us all to see how homophobic and misogynistic hate crime is casually occurring on our streets. Like Rosa Parks before them these women on the bus used a human tale of an everyday incident to speak up. Without that photograph, even with the use of social media, it would have taken a huge and organized campaign to make such a striking point so clearly.

Social media has almost unlimited potential – but

be aware that without savvy use of content, it will not solve all your problems or lead to the change you want to see.

A CAUTIONARY TALE

EVERY DAY THE FIRST thing I do when I wake up is check my phone, private messages, email then Twitter. Today was no different. On my Twitter feed this morning was a public message that directly copied me in with a video filmed in the cloakroom in a school in the area I represent. The message was apparently from the father of a boy who featured in the video, asking me to watch it. The distressing footage depicts this man's son sitting on a bench surrounded by other pupils who look on as a fellow pupil punches him in the head. The man's son eventually stands up but does not seem to be defending himself. Instead, he turns towards the crowd and the camera says something inaudible as the perpetrator, who can be seen behind him, takes a final blow to his face. The video is less than 30 seconds long but is harrowing to watch.

Accompanying the clip is a message to me, telling me that the boy whom the video shows being beaten up has been suspended from school for what happened. It appears from this short video that in this incident the boy who has been punished was – in this snapshot, at least – the victim.

When I saw the video, I looked at the profile of the man who sent it to me and he had just two followers on Twitter. I responded by asking him to contact me directly and privately with the details so I could learn more about what was actually happening here. I did this in good faith and with no other way of communicating with him. By interacting with me and by tagging me in his post, the possible platform of his tweet grew. Within hours of this video being sent to me it had been viewed 100,000 times. Hundreds of messages follow in a thread asking me to help this family and stand up for what is right and just. Within the hour two local news outlets had joined in the conversation and had asked the father to contact them and tell his side of the story, and three had been in touch with me asking for comment. Thirty seconds of video, 180 characters of text and a demand on a local politician had elevated what would have previously been handled in parent–teacher meetings, or through email exchanges, into a public crisis for all involved. But was sharing this video with me in this way the right thing to do? Did it achieve the results that the father was after?

If the father had simply emailed this clip to me, as his local representative, rather than posting it online and tagging me, I would have had an equally horrified response. Whether it was public or not, I would have aimed to act as an honest broker between the school and the family, and sought to hear the full story of what had happened and reach a conclusion that could end with the boy safely back in school.

From the video I can see only a fraction of what has gone on and I certainly don't know the full facts. So I'm on the back foot straight away. And yet, now the narrative has gone public. Who owns it? Certainly not me. The parent? Perhaps he doesn't either. The train is running away down the track, with no one driving.

Social media can be incredibly powerful, especially when using video content, but it's like a super-power: you really have to use it with great care and thought.

In this situation, the school cannot and should not respond or publicly vilify any of its pupils. Even if they have perfectly legitimate explanations within the normal and expected parameters of what goes on in inner-city schools where fights break out and discipline must be managed carefully. Does the action of making this public change the outcome? Have people made judgements about any of the pupils or the school without being in possession of all the facts? It's a very tricky situation. I can't help feeling that this is not the best way to use social media and I hope it doesn't play out badly for any of those involved.

The idea of the citizen as a journalist has undoubtedly meant that wrongdoing, criminality and oppression are harder to hide. But we must be careful how we use this new freedom in the fight to right wrongs. The outcome you seek might come more quickly with this method but it is more difficult for you to control and manage once the media, both modern and traditional, is involved. The question we always have to ask is: does our public action affect the outcome and does it affect it well?

———

This kind of fighting back can have the effect of napalm, scorching the earth all around the issue. It is for this reason that I would suggest it as a last resort or a threat in a battle rather than the opening gambit. If, for example, you are living in damp and unsanitary social housing, I would first try going through the landlord to get something done. If you are ignored and let down, then go up the hierarchy to the local politicians or senior officers in charge. If you are still left in completely crappy living conditions then a compelling video of your home or a chat with the local press may very well stick a rocket up the arse of those who should have done something in the first place. You are armed with the evidence of inaction by the powerful and you have been left with nowhere else to go.

Remember that the cover-up is usually a more compelling story that the original complaint.

If you are going to name and shame people who may have very clearly wronged you, once you say it publicly you had better be able to back it up with evidence and be willing to stand by it in court if they challenge you. You may be telling the truth, but believe me when I say that the truth will not always protect you if you are up against powerful people with expensive lawyers. I cannot tell you how many times I have written and then deleted angry tweets about gropey multi-million-pound bosses that I have heard about because many of their staff have reached out to me to tell me how they are being silenced. If I had pointed the finger publicly at every single politician or businessman I have heard awful stories about, you can bet your bottom dollar I would be penniless through litigation, even if every word I said was true.

This is why journalists have training and learn about the law and ethics. Holding people to account publicly works, but doing it without thought, strategy, evidence and a robust defence can harm both you and your cause.

I am not for a second saying that you shouldn't use social media to call time on bullshit. It's an incredible tool to do just that. I am just saying it is better to properly plan for it and to the best of your ability to plan for all the possible outcomes of doing it.

How will you feel if people lose their jobs – and not always the people you think should lose their jobs?

How will you cope if those you wanted to highlight respond, or if their families do?

Are you prepared to back up what you have said?

Have you got a team of people ready to help you if your moment of anger is seen by a million people in a day?

The moment you press send will always feel like a delicious act of defiance, but I have felt the cold sweat of fear myself when the retweets mount up and the phone rings with messages from journalists, and I realize that I am no longer controlling this. Attention is always needed to get a ball rolling and build momentum for a cause, but attention can be all-consuming and terrifying.

Before you press send, be sure you're ready for it. And at the very least know what your next move might be.

CONNECTING PEOPLE

THE GREATEST POWER that media attention gives to someone speaking up is the ability to connect you with others in the same situation. Every single one of the campaigners I have spoken to for this book has cited social media's ability to swiftly reach other people who want to be part of the effort. An entire industry has sprung out of online activism; there are few people in the UK who have not signed at least one online petition or bunged a few quid to campaign crowdfunding platforms. Crowdfunding for political change or to take legal action has become a permanent pillar in the resistance against the establishment, with political figures like Barack Obama and Alexandria Ocasio-Cortez making a virtue of being funded by a crowd of people rather than by the rich lobbies that dominate American politics. Every single political campaign I have led, including the one to get me elected to parliament, has been largely funded through crowdfunding online. Most recently, in a single week I raised £10,000 to fund a campaign in the capital, where hundreds of schoolchildren will gather at our parliament to fight back against education cuts that mean schools (including my son's own school) will no longer be able to stay open five days a week. The use of crowdfunding platforms not only assists us in raising funds, but also acts to spread the message of the campaign beyond those directly involved.

There is a pitfall to reaching people through social media and petition sites, and that is over-saturation. There are already terms to deride it, such as 'Clicktivism', which suggests that simply clicking on a link or retweeting a video is a minimal effort in the resistance. Politicians regularly mock the latest petition doing the rounds, especially when they are so often signed repeatedly by the same people.

I worry that this democratizing of activism online lures campaigners into a false sense of security. Social media should absolutely be used as a tool to connect you with others who care about an issue or to find the testimony of others who might have been slighted by the same person or organization as you, but alone its overuse risks it being easy for the powerful to ignore.

In any campaign, consider the power of social media to connect you with others to be its main function rather than directly being the end solution.

It needs to be used as part of a plan.

The UK parliament now has a specific Petitions Committee and any parliamentary petition signed by more than 100,000 people will be rewarded with a debate in parliament. I have seen how these petitions and subsequent debates and inquiries by the Petitions Committee have created real changes – but I have also seen how they can lead nowhere.

I was involved with one inquiry that was brought about by a petition started online, following an online story. Nicola Thorp was hired as receptionist at city accountancy firm PwC by the firm Portico who supply agency temp staff in London, and when she arrived for work she was told that she must wear high heels. When she turned up in flat shoes she was sent home without pay. Because obviously women are just dolls who sit at the front desks of businesses to look pretty for their clients.

According to Nicola's temp agency at the time, a two- to four-inch heel was vital for answering the phone, which makes me think I have been using my shoes wrong for years, and that men in flat shoes must not be able to answer phones or open post at all. Nicola initially used Facebook to tell her story and there she found other women with stories to tell. She realized that she was on to something bigger than her own incident. She set up a petition using the UK parliament petition site and told her story through the mainstream media to gather momentum for her petition, which called for a specific action: 'Make it illegal for a company to require women to wear high heels at work.'

The petition was signed by 152,420 people. Nicola also reached out to politicians like me who she thought would back up her call at the same time the petition was running. The petition, the attention and Nicola's lobbying brought the issue to parliament and instead of just getting a debate on the floor of the house (which could have easily then been forgotten), her activism brought about an inquiry of two parliamentary committees. These went on to find evidence of wide-scale practice of women being told that they had to have their hair dyed a certain colour or they had to wear a regulation amount of make-up with a rota for reapplying, regardless of how it affected their performance at the task in hand.

Two years after Nicola had been sent home from work without pay, the joint committees in parliament released a report stating that the temp agency that had insisted on the sexist dress code had broken the law. The report recommended that the existing law needed to be toughened up to end the practice of turning women into dolls. I mean, it didn't say those exact words because parliament rarely speaks like people, but that's what it meant. I know, I was on the committee. The temp company changed its policies and Nicola's action will have been a shot across the bow to anyone who was thinking of demanding women wear high heels at work. This is how to do it well and use social media to rally people and inform change.

IT WILL TAKE MORE THAN JUST CLICKS

FOR EVERY EXAMPLE where the petitions system in parliament and through other activism sites has managed to change the law, there are 20 examples of where the petition fails to inform any real change. In the UK 10,000 signatures means the government must respond, but believe me when I say the government responding usually means it telling the petitioner that it hasn't done anything wrong and is going to change nothing. Here are a few examples of the government responding to online petitions:

Petition: a Public inquiry into disenfranchisement of EU27 citizens and UK citizens abroad

The government responded on 13 June 2019:

'The government took all the legal steps necessary and put in place all the legislative and funding elements to enable Returning Officers to carry out their statutory duties for the 23 May polls.'

So basically, thousands of citizens missed out on their opportunity to vote and were turned away at the ballot box because they were born in a different country, which is a really fucking serious charge. The government just responds and says, 'Oh well, nothing to see here.'

Or this one:

Petition: Re-instate nursing bursary and scrap tuition fees

The government responded on 14 May 2019:

'The tuition fee model means universities can offer more nursing places and students can access more funding than under the bursary system, and there are no plans to reinstate the bursary.'

The government's response to a petition highlighting how the number of people undertaking nursing training has fallen as a direct result of its policy to end funding to support these students is, basically, 'You are wrong; go away.'

The government is not scared of the petition itself and, without a broader campaign, can easily brush off such efforts, in the process belittling and patronizing the people involved, in these cases citizens in the UK born in the European Union and nurses. This is the very definition of bullshit.

Online platforms to raise money and support for a cause are brilliant tools, but without other events, attention, legal challenges and dedicated political support, they will not shift the powerful to action. Without question they should be used, and it is really exciting for the hospital porter or the local school class to watch as the number of signatures on their petition racks up, but it takes more than just a petition to change things.

CONTENT IS KING

TRYING TO GET public interest in a campaign that doesn't just rely on controversy is not easy. I know, as someone who receives thousands of emails every week from one of the many petition sites campaigners use. Running campaigns is a crowded field, which makes getting traction harder. Just a quick scan through the emails I have received today: *Please support pubs and help cut beer duty*; *1 million children trapped in Idlib, Syria*; *Pledge to protect our rivers.* Good press coverage or compelling social media content will change your campaign from a bureaucratic petition into activism with momentum.

You must think about what you can do that will stand out and get noticed, and you have to ensure that you build on that throughout your efforts to change things. This goes back to the idea of storytelling and how important it is to have a compelling story well told. Often the things I seek to change involve very vulnerable people who might not feel able – or, in fact, be able – to pose for photos and videos. I know from working with victims of sexual violence that when you are trying to get attention for a campaign about how rape crisis centres are being cut, or how the courts are failing victims the first thing the press will ask is, 'Can you get me a victim to speak on camera?' This is almost always a hard no, so we have had to think of other ways to highlight the facts that would be compelling. Making videos of other women giving voice to the words of victims, using animation and creating infographics to show the statistics on the number of rape victims failed in court are some examples of trying to tell the story so people can see it and easily understand it.

The campaigners working to repeal the Eighth Amendment in the Irish Constitution, which barred abortions in the country, faced the same challenges of vulnerability and confidentiality. However, the campaigners from the London-Irish Abortion Rights Campaign planned very creative events of storytelling that would win them the attention of the media and provide content for social-media campaigning all in one.

In 2016, before it was even announced that Ireland would hold a referendum on their abortion laws, the London-Irish Abortion Rights Campaign organized for 77 women to gather and then march around the block of the Irish embassy in London. Each of the women brought along a suitcase on wheels to pull along as they marched. Without needing women to come forward about their abortions, these 77 women and their 77 suitcases represented the number of women recorded each week who travel from Ireland to the UK to have an abortion. The women marched in a line passed the embassy. The campaigners had used social media to gather people to their protest and also to inform any interested media that they would be there. On that day a photo was captured of these women in an act of silent protest and that image would go on to symbolize the referendum campaign.

In an interview in the *Independent* newspaper after the referendum result was announced, the photographer who took the iconic image, Alastair Moore, said:

'I brought my camera to the protest at the Irish embassy in London by chance. The crowd grew quickly at the meeting spot and the organizers lined all the women up double file with their luggage to represent the Irish women forced to travel to the UK for abortions.

'They set off on a march around the block, passing the embassy. When they started moving, the sound of the luggage wheels on the footpath was deafening. It was incredibly impactful – it had this feeling of a growing momentum and anger at injustice, but it was so civil.

'They did one lap of the block and I realized I had to catch a shot of them coming around the corner.

It wasn't until I got home that I realized that every single woman had the same determined look on their face. A really powerful scene to witness.'

Throughout the referendum campaign the image taken by Alastair Moore went viral and was seen hundreds of thousands of times all around the world. This was not an accident; the creativity of the campaign had been designed exactly for this reason. Powerful images matter when campaigning for change. Cara Sanquest told me: 'Our audience, when we were organizing all of those protests, was international media. We were always trying to get in the *New York Times* or the English press. We were trying to get attention and make it everyone's shame not just the women who have to travel, not just an Irish problem that it's dealing with on its own. We wanted the world to see.'

Clever and creative content in any campaign will make you stand out from those who just wave placards. It will create images that tell the story and then be shared again and again on social media. It will give the newspapers you need to multiply your reach an angle to the story. I was told early on in my political career that the mantra for most media outlets is: 'Fill the fucking space.'

In an era of 24-hour news and minute-by-minute online output, news organizations need stuff to write about; if you make it interesting they will report it.

A rally on its own is not a news story, not unless you get a million people to turn up. Similarly, a protest outside a building is not very newsworthy; there needs to be an interesting and creative angle. Lots of campaigns use famous faces to grab attention, so if you are mates with Angelina Jolie, bravo, you'll probably make the headlines. If you aren't, then you will need to think about how you can tell your story in the quickest and most interesting way.

WHO ARE YOU TALKING TO?

WHEN YOU ARE creating media content you need to think about who you are talking to and what you are trying to achieve with your powerful video or online petition. A common mistake of campaigns is not having a clear idea of who you are addressing. If you have lived through the years of Brexit hell in the UK, or the pro-Trump—anti-Trump division in America, you will have plenty of examples of people speaking on platforms about how right they are and how wrong everyone else is. This simply turns people off and feeds into the feral environment of both social and mainstream media. In the UK both the leave and the remain campaigns have, since the referendum result, aimed their messaging at the people who already agree with them. Most of the British public have checked out of the debate and frankly just want it to end. This style of messaging is a totally pointless exercise in enjoying the sound of your own voice and kissing your guns at how great you are.

Preaching to the choir is not speaking truth to power, it is useless.

The other common mistake that campaigners make, myself included, is to talk only to the people who completely disagree with them. (What can I say? Sometimes it is too bloody tempting.) Being much better than your opponent is delicious, but having loads of content that proves how wrong they are and therefore how right you are will only get you so far. People with hardened positions will never change their minds. Those people will never agree with you, and you are wasting your time trying to get them to. Climate activists will never convince climate change deniers that carbon is killing our planet;

likewise, climate deniers will never manage the reverse.

Very occasionally, preaching to the choir or skewering your ultra-opposition with a sick burn will help bolster your supporters and keep them going, but to make this your main messaging or your main audience is nothing more than an indulgence doomed to failure.

If you want to change things you have to build up a critical mass of the people who can be convinced. People often mistakenly think that when politicians go door to door during election campaigns, we are there selling our message and trying to change minds. Long debates on the doorstep with dissenters are a waste of time; what we are doing is talking to the people who are unsure and finding out where the people who are with us are, so we can call on them when we need them.

Targeting the people whom you want to reach when using blunt tools like Twitter, Facebook and YouTube or the news media can be a minefield. You will inevitably reach people who don't agree with you, who will try to draw you into long time-wasting arguments.

Again, don't fall down the rabbit hole! Remember, the outcome you are aiming for is not to change the mind of Allan in Sidcup, it's to fight for equal pay or miners' pensions; ignore Allan in Sidcup, he's not with you.

Facebook will allow you to target your content at specific geographical locations or people who are interested in certain things. It is a tool that exists and if you wish to use Facebook to target people in a certain area or of a certain demographic you can do this for relatively small amounts of money. So, if you wanted to find a group of Muslim women in your area to join a campaign about workplace discrimination for Muslim women, you could do it.

This approach is not wholly accurate, as any young woman who has ever been push marketed incontinence pants or menopause meds will know, but at least you're getting closer to the right people.

When deciding to try to change something, think about who you need to convince and lean on them. The Grenfell survivors, for example, are at the stage in their long-term campaign where the people they need to change housing regulation are the country's politicians, so they use the methods of getting people to contact their individual representative and putting pressure on them to push the government. They have also very creatively projected onto the side of tower blocks across the UK their demands and the ways in which the government are currently failing. They know who they are targeting, and they are speaking to an audience who they know will help them push their target.

Cara Sanquest expressed this better than most when describing to me how in the Irish referendum campaign they focused entirely on people who were undecided or unsure. 'What we realized in the referendum was that turnout was going to matter. The people who were going to vote "No" to the change were always going to vote that way, no matter what we did. An increase in turnout wasn't going to help their campaign but to us it was going to make the difference.' They did not fall into the trap of trying to win a fight with pro-life campaigners, no matter how much they were provoked. They realized that they needed people who were either unsure or living away from home to vote. So, they launched the Home to Vote campaign, which sought to bring Irish people back from around the world to vote to repeal the Eighth Amendment. They made focused and targeted video content and fed stories to the media about people making long journeys home to Ireland to vote to give freedom and safety to Irish women. The message was very powerful and emotional because the imagery of people travelling to vote, especially from England, once again leaned on the imagery of women having to travel to get safe abortions. The Home to Vote campaign was not just powerful, it was also very clever and designed to target the right audience. In putting out videos of people setting off on long journeys from the US, Canada and Japan the week before the vote, they were also sending a message to those at home who thought they might not bother to just walk down the road. 'Because we knew the journey would start a couple of days before the vote, that really bolstered our voter mobilization in Ireland. If some people had to start planning three days before the poll, people at home would be, like, "Shit, I can walk ten minutes to my polling station."' It was talking not to the passionate pro-choicer or the ardent pro-lifer, but to the dispassionate and disaffected.

The social media output on the week of the referendum linked by the hashtag #hometovote was some of the most powerful campaign content I have ever seen:

> **I'm coming #hometovote! Will be travelling**
> **5,169 miles from LA to Dublin and will be**
> **thinking of every Irish woman who has had to**
> **travel to access healthcare that should be available**

> in their own country. Let's do this, Ireland!
> #hometovote from Queensland to Dublin.
> Arrived in today and worth it. Drinking Lyons
> tea at 5am with jetlag.

The images of people travelling and the messages from across the world reached out to those who were not directly affected. Where I live in Birmingham, myself and others were offering lifts or money to get people on plains and ferries, and we were not the only ones: all week social media was full of similar stories.

> Just landed in Dublin and picked up my rental car.
> If you or anyone you know needs a lift to a polling
> station hit me up. I can't promise I can get to
> everyone, but I'll do my best. #hometovote

> A friend of mine wasn't allowed to fly from
> Manchester as she forgot her passport. Random
> stranger in the airport transferred her 400 pounds
> to book flights tomorrow morning. She will be
> #hometovote. I will be crying.

The Home to Vote campaign should be our touch-stone in the use of the media to inform change. It did not seek to shame, it sought to change and inspire. The campaigners used creative, inclusive content to spread their message and they were clear about who they were talking to. When using social media or the mainstream press, always be clear what outcome it is that you seek. Be prepared to handle the attention it can bring and have a clear idea of who you are trying to reach.

———

So, use the media to connect with people, to persuade and gather voices as part of a defined plan – and you will likely prosper in your cause. If you use it only to attack, expect it to turn people off and to offer ammunition to your opponent. Shaming people in the media should be the last resort, not a first resort, because lasting change rarely comes from a scalp. Use all the modern tools at your disposal to find stories, rally troops and inspire change, but be wary that without thought and planning you might start a fire that you cannot put out.

KEEP GOING
AND
ENJOY IT

THE FIRST TIME you speak up, even if it is over some seemingly small thing, like intervening on the bus when you can see some drunk bloke is bothering the woman sat next to him, or picking up litter dropped by a passer-by and pacing up to them and telling them they dropped something, your heart will race and your skin will prickle. The next time you do it you will find it a fraction easier, and then each time after that the pattern will continue until eventually you will stop thinking twice. You will have changed.

Speaking up about stuff that is wrong is not an innate

skill; it is not something that even those with the big-gest voices and bravest reputations find easy. I certainly don't, but practice has taught me how to approach dif-ferent situations and how to assess if my voice will cause resolution or trouble. I don't wade into things if I think my intervention will make things more difficult to resolve, but I don't use that as an excuse for inaction either.

Practice, as with anything, makes us better. Every single one of the people I interviewed or have written about in this book are ordinary people who did some-thing to fight back and, in the process, trained themselves for the next thing. None of the have-a-go heroes, activ-ists, campaigners or bereaved family members saw their injustice in isolation or wasted the skills they learned tackling it, merely chalking it up to experience. Activism and righteousness are infectious and moreish.

When you see that it can be done, I guarantee you will want to do it again. You will start to enjoy it.

Zelda Perkins has turned initial courage into practical lobbying, not only of politicians and the legal industry, but also of the institutions that regulate how the law is practised. She has used the voice she always had, before it was silenced, to tell the story far and wide to help change the way that employment law treats women in the workplace. Twenty-five years of waiting to see her case come out in the open did not squash her desire to do the right thing.

Paul Caruana Galizia and his brothers have picked up the mantle left by their mother following her assassination. If anyone had a right to feel cowed by their experiences it is them, and yet they are working with lawyers and politicians to continue to fight the corruption that killed Daphne. Paul is now working as an investigative journalist, shining a light on other issues of corruption himself.

Sara Rowbotham, sacked from her job working directly with the girls she sacrificed herself to protect, was not deterred by her experience. In 2015 she stood for election on behalf of the labour party for her local council in Rochdale, the very institution she had been forced to take on. Sara was duly elected by the good people of that town. Now deputy leader and in charge of health and wellbeing on the council, she spends her life trying to improve the institutions she originally set out to challenge.

Cara Sanquest, the abortion rights campaigner who helped to change history for women in Ireland, is still using her amazing organizing skills alongside her sisters in the London-Irish Abortion Rights Campaign to fight for a similar law change for the women of Northern Ireland. She now works in the UK parliament for the MP Stella Creasy and dedicates much of her time, both in work and outside, to find a way to make abortion free, safe and legal for women the world over.

Natasha Elcock of Grenfell United is still very much living amid her campaign to improve the lives of people in social housing. At my most recent meeting with her in parliament, she was as usual using the skills she has learned along the way. When previously she may have been shrunk by meetings in fancy buildings, I watched how she did not falter in talking back to politicians attempting to placate her or offer up flannel instead of actions. I have no doubt that once Natasha sees the law changes she is struggling for come to fruition, she will not simply go back to the way things were, she will be using her experiences to fight for even further change for even more people.

———

Tom Watson, of course, was already a politician when he took on one of the most powerful institutions in the world, the Murdoch press, but even in him the change is marked from before and after. He continues to take on the hard cases with powerful lobbies, such as the gambling lobby, which he has recently fought back against in a campaign to reduce the amount of money that can be poured into fixed-odds betting machines by the poor and vulnerable. His willingness to speak out about problems within his own political party on anti-Semitism and bullying is brave. It is difficult, but he does it wearing the amour of a man who has taken on much worse and faced a far scarier backlash.

It was a genuine honour and a privilege to sit and chat with each of these now well-practised crusaders. Their stories were all different, and the outcomes of their actions varied, but the single thing that they had in common was that none of them thought they were special or brave. They all balked at the idea that they had done something that was out of the ordinary. Funnily enough, they all cited other people who they thought were the real heroes of their stories. For Paul this was his mother, but I am certain she would say the same about him taking on her crusade. All mentioned the victims who had come forward, the neighbours who had helped, the brave people willing to share their stories, the journalists who had taken a risk to help them. They cited their fellow campaigners and the people who had stuck with them, their team, their comrades. None wanted to own their successes or courage alone.

These people are now skilful campaigners. I wanted to pass on the benefit of their years of practice so I asked each one of the people I interviewed: 'If you could give one piece of advice to someone who was thinking about speaking up or starting a campaign to change things, what would it be?' This is what they said:

Zelda Perkins

Trust people and don't be afraid to ask for help. For people who speak up or get put in a position where they have to speak up, it is quite a lonely thing to do. I have drawn strength from myself – and that drove me. When you do speak to power and power fucks you over, you lose a lot of trust, but you do have to try and trust people otherwise you can't ask for help.

Paul Caruana Galizia

This quote is from one of my mother's Sunday columns in the *Malta Independent*, which was published on 3 March

2013, the day before Joseph Muscat (current Prime Minister) was first elected. The headline was 'Do what is right'.

> I cannot bear the thought of injustice, still less the reality of it. It's true that life is unfair and that much of it can't be helped, but where I can do anything to avoid unfairness or to set it straight, then I will.
>
> There are situations which create so much disillusionment that they can seriously undermine our faith in human nature, in the hope that good will triumph over bad, that people will get what they deserve, that those who don't deserve things won't get them, that fortune will favour the brave and not the unworthy. Evidence all around us that this does not necessarily happen can make us angry. But rather than giving in to anger or disillusionment, it is better, and more consoling, to know that we have done our best to avert the triumph of the undeserving, in which those who have served us ill are rewarded while those who have served well are punished.

Tom Watson MP

Obviously, I encourage people to do it. Try to establish your support network before you do it. If you're in a union, or if you're in a community group, or faith group, or you've got people you know can help, take advice before you do it. Be meticulous in documenting events. I'm a person who has actually failed in that, but keep records of everything. There will be advice out there. You might have to spend a bit of time finding it but you must do all you can to protect yourself; power will go to extreme depths.

Sara Rowbotham

Remember that you know what's right and what's wrong. Don't be intimidated by people's position or a perceived superior knowledge or experience. Because actually, if you know you're right, then right is might. You do have to somehow be resourceful and keep going, not waver; to do that, find who your ally is and who your rock is. To me, your ally is like a critical friend, it's somebody who is able to say, 'Have you thought about this or that?' That helps you be a lot clearer in your own head. Sometimes your rock will be slightly different to an ally

– it's somebody who loves you unconditionally and can keep you going. If you've got those things it will stabilize you. Unfortunately, anger is a real motivator. I was more and more angry every day. I probably didn't channel the anger always in the right way, but if you can use that it's like fire in your belly, it keeps you going somehow.

Natasha Elcock

Don't be afraid of the system. The reason I say that is because now I understand the system. I understand how this bloody country works and it is not as clear-cut as it may seem. It's not as fancy. I could talk to MPs all day long, especially those in government; they all come with a bunch of civil servants. Up until this point, I promise you I didn't realize how it worked. I don't know what planet I've been living on, but I thought, like most people, that the Prime Minister was in charge, that they make all the decisions. But I realize now that they have loads of people around them in the civil service and special advisors; they need people advising them, they need people like us telling them what's what. I've never really been into politics, but if I'd known that's how things worked I would have been afraid to stand up against the politician, thinking that they have this immense power. So don't let what you think is happening stop you speaking up. Grenfell United has taught me that as a group we definitely have more power than we thought.

Cara Sanquest

My one piece of advice might be a boring one, but try not to do it on your own. I've never felt alone in any of this work. There's a whole army of people who always wanted to change this. I don't know how you keep going if you're doing it on your own.

Get people involved and keep people involved. Give people autonomy, give them a structured space to come up with ideas, and give them a lot of support to deliver those ideas. Find out people's skills and use them, but most important is to keep people coming back.

TAKE THE POWER BACK

SPEAKING TRUTH to power is not a one-off – it often becomes a lifestyle. If you've done it once, you usually cannot stop. So how can you step up to the next level?

I am obviously biased about this, but I always ask the same question of every one of the people I have met who bravely took on an establishment, : 'Have you ever thought of running for political office?' I know this is not for everyone, I get that, but I look around at those in political office across the world and I know how much better the world would be if the humble everyday campaigners were the ones running it.

I understand that not everyone can become a politician when they don't like what is happening in their area or to their people. I'm not suggesting that they should, but I do think that those of us who get a taste for campaigns and speaking up should consider trying their hand and trying to take up space in powerful places. We should not always let the same old faces wield all the power. Most companies, charities and organizations have governance structures that you can seek to influence, and if you can't influence the people on them, try to become one of them. If the company that you work for has bad workplace practices, you could get together with your colleagues and set up a union branch and elect your own reps, for example. If you don't like disciplinary policies at your kids' school, you can get on the governing body.

If you are worried about the corruption in your local council, stand to be a local councillor. This is not selling out or becoming part of the problem. Think about the 50 councillors who currently sit on Kensington and Chelsea Borough Council; they are the people who oversee standards in social housing in the area where Grenfell Tower burned. Imagine now how different things could be if they were replaced with 50 of the survivors of the tower. Decisions would be different, right?

The world is run by those who turn up. Don't assume that you can't be one of those people or that you don't have the skills or the fancy language to do it. I have been in meetings at almost every single level of power in my country and let me tell you, there is nothing more insightful or cleverer being said in the meetings at the very top than in those at the very bottom. Believe that you have something to offer that might be missing. I have seen how voices missing from the debate are forgotten about and decisions that are made without them are bad.

Of course, for certain groups and demographics there are lots of structural reasons that stop people from being able to take up space. If I look around, for example, at Westminster or Washington, I can see it is a lot easier for posh white men who went to expensive schools to become decision-makers than it is for people like me or you, but that will always be the case if people don't put themselves forward. The world is changing, and authentic voices have a far greater power to shift the status quo than blokes in suits, but you do have to turn up.

You don't have to be a massive crusader, a politician or a policy lead at a national charity, you can use your voice to change the way things work in your world just by not being a bystander to bullshit and offering up an hour of your time to join in and help someone trying to do the right thing. We have much more power than people think; I wish we would use it. If we don't use our voices and make decisions for ourselves, dark forces pretending to speak for us will do it and pretend that we asked for it. I am frequently being told by right-wing political voices that the white working classes in the Midlands and the north in my country, or the working men in the rust belt of America, all agree with the populist racist policies of Donald Trump and Nigel Farage. I am told repeatedly that people like me who defend women's rights and multicultural policies of equality and diversity are letting down these working-class men and that they hate people like me. Then I spend my weekends in the pub with my husband – a white working-class bloke without a degree, who has a manual job – and his mates from the building site, and they don't seem to hate me or think I am letting them down. They also, by and large, don't know that their voices are being hijacked by rich, powerful men to make their point. If you don't use your voice or think you have the power to, I guarantee you someone – be it your boss, your local representative or your president – will pretend that they speak for you whether you like it or not. If people felt they knew how to get their own voice heard, or thought that it would be worthwhile bothering, it would be much harder for people with power to simply speak for them with such disregard for the reality or the facts.

BELIEVE THAT YOU CAN CHANGE THINGS AND ENJOY IT

I KNOW THERE is a risk that this has all got a bit heavy and you might be thinking, I am not sure that I can take on Google or Facebook's global domination, or bring down corrupt governments in South America. After all, you probably have enough on with work or study, and the washing won't do itself, right? It's a fair point. But I am here to tell you that it doesn't have to be a difficult slog or a lifelong campaign for people to get involved and change things.

The stories we tell to inspire people to speak truth to power are often rooted in sadness, systematic failure and loss. Most people look around at our current global political landscape and utterly despair, feeling certain that things won't change. Even those presenting themselves as change-makers and radicals, from both the left and the right, seem to end up ultimately disappointing us, doing nothing more than trying to hold on to their own powerbase, no matter the cost. Shit happens all the time and we can all feel a bit hopeless; even big, bold, brave broads like me put my head in my hands with despair from time to time. At least once a month I will take to Twitter to provide me with a moment of cheap therapy, to declare how I am losing the will to keep going when nothing ever seems to change. I get it; things are fucking depressing right now.

The very best antidote in the world to this depression, however, is the joy you will feel when you stand alongside a crowd of people, using your voice to try to change things. I am done telling you that speaking truth to power is hard, and can be dangerous and costly, because the truth of why I do it is not only righteousness but also because the feeling I get in my soul when I try is better than any drug in the world.

The morning I am writing this, I have just picked up the *Guardian* newspaper from my local corner shop. Half of the front page is emblazoned with an image of the iconic door to 10 Downing Street. In front of that door sit four ordinary schoolchildren from Kings Heath Primary School in Birmingham. One of the children is my son Danny. Together with hundreds of children from schools across the country, Danny and his classmates went with their parents to the UK capital to demand better funding for their schools. The funding cuts they are protesting against mean that for thousands of children in England their schools will not stay open for five days a week any more. On this Friday afternoon these children should be in school but they can't be because of cuts. These four children sitting on the steps of 10 Downing Street demanding that the government take responsibility for them make it clear in a single image that the powerful in our country have failed to take care of the education of our children. The juxtaposition of four seemingly powerless children sitting in front of the home of power in the UK, just doing their homework, is not only bad press for the powerful, but also beams it out across the country and shouts to all of the families who are also seeing their kids' education damaged.

Hundreds of schoolchildren and parents, many who are not particularly political and certainly wouldn't describe themselves as activists, got up at 6am on the morning of the protest, explained to their bosses that they wouldn't be at work that day, made arrangements for their other children, got on coaches in the blazing heat and travelled with noisy, excitable children for hours to get to London. On arrival, they gathered in front of the Houses of Parliament and sang songs with the children, mixed with people just like them from across the country, and together marched to the home of our Prime Minister. As the protest gathered outside the gates of Downing Street, hundreds of voices of children aged four to eleven sang out, 'No ifs, no buts, no education cuts.' We were not sure if we were going to be allowed to take children from the protest behind the gates, but en masse we waited and chanted, thrilled to be there together to make our point. An armed police officer approached and opened a side gate and spoke quietly to me to say that four of the children would be allowed in to deliver a petition and present their demands. The four children pushed their way through the crowd and, accompanied by myself and the police officer, entered the enclosure that protects the heart of the UK government. Through the big iron gates, the gathered protestors could see as these four ten-year olds proceeded up the famous terraced street. As the children slowly made their way, the roar from the protestors rose to such a crescendo that even the memory of it is bringing tears to my eyes. The feeling of euphoria amongst the crowd, that we as citizens could rally together, join WhatsApp groups, raise a few quid, go to meetings and make the effort to get our arses down to a place of such iconic power, was palpable. People in the crowd started to hug each other and felt genuine swelling pride that we were not just going to sit back and be ignored. We were doing shit to stop the shit.

I have no idea if my little boy and his friends and their protest will change the crappy situation they are in at their school. I hope it does, but in that moment it didn't matter if we would win or not. In that moment our children still faced an uncertain future with reduced education. The bad thing that depressed us was still there, but for the hundreds of people on that protest with their kids, what mattered was that they tried, they didn't give up and accept their lot. You have no idea how good that feels. It feels like love and hope and possibility.

Speaking truth to power will often mean quite a lot of work and organizing. It can feel like a long slog, and a painful process but, a bit like pregnancy and childbirth, the moment of euphoria makes you forget all of the shit bits. It might sound glib for me to say that you will enjoy it, but you will feel camaraderie like you have never felt before and you will be left, even in unsuccessful campaigns, thinking that you can make a difference. Speaking truth to power is often really enjoyable, not just the pay-offs, not just the big moments, but the process of working with other people to try to do something that you have devised yourself is like soul food. Some of the best times of my life have been sat crying with tears of laughter late at night with a bunch of misfits who would never normally be together while we stuff another few thousand envelopes to lobby a local neighbourhood to join us. Trying to do something no matter how bloody mad it might be is genuinely fun.

This is equally true of the smaller acts of resistance that might just be you refusing to be a bystander to bad stuff. Even when I have had a mouthful of abuse from a dickhead after telling them that in fact the whole train carriage doesn't want to listen to their gabber techno and they should turn it off, I feel good about it. I bet every single person has listened to the story about how one of their mates put the workplace bully in their place or broke up a fight outside the pub and gave everyone a good talking-to. The reason these stories get told is because people feel proud of themselves for standing up to nonsense. They want to tell you because they want to prolong the enjoyment that they feel from having tried to make the world a bit better. Speaking truth to power is not just about puritanical selfless good deeds of the über-righteous; people would just give up if it wasn't in some way enjoyable, soothing or therapeutic. Even in the most adverse circumstances it is okay to feel good about yourself and enjoy trying to change things. When a government minister rings me to tell me that they are going to meet the demands I am making on a particular policy, even when it is about something as depressing as rape convictions, I get this immense adrenaline rush and a bursting feeling in my chest at the joy that bothering to try was worth it. I often have to keep it secret from the people I have campaigned with and for, because of some press embargo or another, and so I spend a lot of time on the phone to my husband explaining intricate government policy that he largely doesn't understand or care about just so I can end by saying, 'We won.' Pride does not always come before a fall; often it is the thing that will push us through to get on with the next thing. You have got to try to enjoy speaking truth to power if you intend to make a habit of it. Trust me, there are plenty of heart-bursting, face-aching-with-happiness, whole-body-cartwheeling moments of joy to be had for just giving a shit enough to do something.

———

You have more power than you think; don't give it away to people who don't deserve it.

LET'S USE IT.

ACKNOWLEDGEMENTS

This is my favourite bit of the book-writing process, the thank you part. First of all, thank you to Jake Lingwood, my editor, who found, as everyone always does, that I am quick to say yes to everything, including writing this book, but because I say yes to everything I'm incredibly hard to work with and am rarely available. He gave me sound advice, made me believe I could do it and accepted that the life of a politician is basically an unpredictable mess. To Laura Macdougall, my agent, who made me write stuff in the first place. Every word I write is thanks to her pestering me to meet her for a cup of coffee. She is always on my side. Thanks also to Caroline Brown, Matt Grindon, Sophie Elletson, Geoff Fennell and Pete Hunt at Octopus; and George Moore, Amelia Knight and Kate Appleton at Midas PR for all your brilliant hard work on the book, and dealing with all the book-world stuff I don't understand.

The greatest thanks has to go to the people who I interviewed for the book, the speakers of truth. Every time I felt as if I couldn't write any more I would listen back to their interviews and was immediately inspired to keep going. Each of them has no idea what rock stars they are; to me, they are pin-ups. Some have suffered terrible loss and lifelong trauma, and still what strikes me when I listen back to the recordings is how much we laughed together and felt hopeful together. Every single one of them gossiped with me and requested that the recording was stopped at some point. I will keep those secrets. Thank you to Zelda Perkins, Paul Caruana-Galizia, Tom Watson, Sara Rowbotham, Natasha Elcock and Cara Sanquest for helping me write this book, but also for making the world a better place.

Thanks to Isobel Housecroft for going through my Twitter to find abusive tweets about me to use as examples, because there are only so many times I can trawl through people abusing me before I start to go mad.

Thanks as always to my husband Tom and my sons Harry and Danny. They have to sacrifice so much of me to causes and crusades that it is a bit much to sacrifice me to book writing as well. They did it mostly with grace and support, although I have definitely been dishing out more guilt money and sweets than normal – to the kids that is, not Tom, he just stoically puts up with it. Thanks, Tom.

Finally, thanks to my Dad for telling me since the day I was born that no one in the world is better than anyone else and everyone's voice matters.